Praise for:

Financial $trategies For Women: The Basics

"*Financial Strategies For Women:* **The Basics** is an excellent 'mini encyclopedia' on all financial matters we are faced with in our adult years. The chapters on mortgages, car and house insurance and credit ratings are especially helpful. They provide detailed information that is easy to understand and follow."

Gail Furlan, M.S.W., C.S.W
Social Work Administrator,
Children's Aid Society, Sarnia, Ontario

"An excellent resource; every woman will benefit from this book."

Pat Kirkby, B.Sc.N., M.A.
Dean, Health Sciences & Human Services
Fanshawe College, London, Ontario

"Women need to actively participate in planning their financial futures. *Financial Strategies For Women:* **The Basics** provides an excellent source of information and reference to lessen the intimidation caused by lack of financial planning knowledge."

Bev Middlemass
Brokerage Manager
Transamerica Life Insurance Company of Canada
Markham, Ontario

Financial $trategies For Women

THE BASICS

Financial $trategies For Women

THE BASICS

Shirley D. Neal
Sherrye E. Emery
Jacqueline A. Papke

W.I.N. (Women's Investment Network) Inc.

Canadian Cataloguing in Publication Data

Neal, Shirley., 1938–
     Financial $trategies for women : the basics

Includes index.
ISBN 0-9698065-0-7

1. Women – Finance, Personal. I. Emery, Sherrye E.
II. Papke, Jacqueline A. III. Women's Investment
Network. IV. Title. V. Title: Financial strategies
for women: the basics.

HG179.N43 1994   332.024'042   C94-930620-7

Printed and Bound in Canada
W.I.N. (Women's Investment Network) Inc.
981 Wellington Rd. S., Suite 402
London, Ontario
N6E 3A9

Cover Design: Michael J. T. Ambroise, Up Yonder Publications.
Computer Layout: Maritza Brikisak, New Dimensions.

SHIRLEY D. NEAL

(B.A., B.Ed., M.Ed., C.F.P.) Vice President of W.I.N. (Women's Investment) Inc., became a Financial Consultant in 1985. Shirley was the Branch Liaison and Training Co-ordinator for a major independent Mutual Fund Broker for three years. She was also a marketing and sales consultant for a variety of companies and organizations.

Shirley has hosted over 60 Cable Television programmes on financial planning and community issues. She was the author of several technical, marketing, sales training, and recruitment manuals and is a member of the Canadian Authors Association.

From 1986 until 1990, Shirley organized and presented seminars in sales and motivation for Anthony Robbins, Robbins Research Institute, during which time she received her Certification as a Neuro Linguistic Programmer.

Shirley's sons, Michael and Stephen live in Ontario, while her daughter, Shelley lives in Alberta.

DEDICATION

Dedicated to Reta Blanche (Downing) Neal. My mother has always been an inspiration in my life. She provided dedication, insight and the attitude that you can attain your dreams by working for them. She is a great example of how to enjoy life, to face your challenges directly and to grow older gracefully. Thanks Mom for all the encouragement you have given me to be all that I can be and to achieve my goals.

Also dedicated to my Aunts Ruth, Inez and Irene who continue to support my ideas, and to my personal cheering section, Michael, Stephen, and Shelley Ambroise.

SHERRYE E. EMERY

President of W.I.N. (Women's Investment Network) Inc. Sherrye has been a Financial Consultant with the Regal Capital Group since 1981 and a District Manager overseeing four offices in Eastern Ontario.

Sherrye's career experience includes banking, construction, the film industry and ownership of a very successful restaurant for over ten years.

As a dedicated member of the Brockville Ad and Sales Club and the Brockville Women's Network, Sherrye works tirelessly in supporting the education and leadership roles of these groups in her community.

Sherrye is a widow with six grown sons and eleven grand children. Her enthusiasm, integrity and professionalism made Sherrye the unanimous choice for President of W.I.N.

DEDICATION

To my mother, Frances Lillian Chillcott, who was my guiding light in my formative years. She was a business woman who combined career and family, giving the best to both. She gave me the confidence and courage to tackle any career, job, problem or task. She taught me how to pack 36 hours of daily work into a 24 hour day.

To my sister, Arline Wright, who is still around to bring me back down to earth every time I start feeling too self important and pleased with my own success.

Also, to all my granddaughters, who I hope will follow my footsteps into the business world.

JACQUELINE A. PAPKE

(B. Admin.) Many years in personnel management, insurance sales and financial consulting has shown Jacquie the crucial need for more financial education.

Jacquie is a LIFE MEMBER of Canada's largest women's organization (C.W.L.). She has been active in politics, serving as trustee on both school boards in the Waterloo Region. These experiences give her firsthand knowledge in understanding the intricacies of Budgets, Tax Structures and Finance.

Currently, Jacquie is Vice President of W.I.N. (Women's Investment Network) Inc. and Vice President and National Manager of Regal Capital Agencies. Jacquie also owns a company which conducts public seminars on financial planning.

Jacquie attributes her success to her husband Lloyd and her family: Gordon; Karen and David Staines, Lauren and Shelley; David and Janet, Jason, James and Katie.

DEDICATION

I dedicate this book to my friend and mother, Evelyn M. (Amundson) (Bell) Wray, whose untiring support helped uncover initiatives I did not know existed. Her Norwegian pioneer spirit has carried through me and my children's generation with boldness, sensitivity, optimism and a sense of humour.

To my grandmothers Anna Amundson and Isabelle Bell, my aunts Alice, Chris, Olga, Vivian Amundson, Florence, Grace and Mary Bell, who remain positive influences in my life. They all proclaimed education, independence and achievement was attainable long before it was in fashion. I dedicate what I have learned to you.

Table of Contents

Acknowledgments

This book is the culmination of effort by many people who compiled information, shared ideas, edited and detected major and minuscule discrepancies when the gremlins got into the computer. Special thanks to our editing and support team: Sharon Sharp, Diz Dichmont, Elva Locklin, Valerie D. Campbell, Eileen Pickering, Phyllis McManus, Amy Burke, Jean Sheridan and Gail Garbett.

To Maritza Brikisak who did all the page layouts. This book would not be published without her dedication, creativity and constant attention to detail. She incorporated all our ideas into the fabric of the final draft.

M. Joy Davis, A.I.I.C., Regal Insurance Brokers gave us her expertise from over 25 years as General Insurance Agent by providing information for Chapters 16 and 17.

We also acknowledge all the people who encouraged, supported and took care of us whether the work was going well or not. Heartfelt thanks to Michael Ambroise, Larry Emery, Ronald F. Goudy, Lloyd Papke, Paul Rockel and Greg Sly. To Eileen 'Jackie' Watson, Maureen Stewart and all those who supported our early efforts, we appreciate your encouragement.

Shirley D. Neal
Sherrye E. Emery
Jacqueline A. Papke

Introduction

"If you don't know where you're going, you will probably end up somewhere else
ANON

If you set out on a journey from St. John's, Newfoundland to Victoria, British Columbia travelling by yourself in a car, how would you prepare for the trip? Would you leave your home without a map, without checking your vehicle for roadworthiness, or the weather; without buying travellers cheques, reserving hotel rooms or notifying friends and relatives along the way when you might be in their area?

Why is it then, another trip most women must face alone at some point in their lives and which usually lasts much longer than the cross country trip, is often taken with less thought and less preparation? The time women spend alone or are financially responsible for themselves and others, whether by choice or not, is much more rigorous! The impact of the consequences are more profound and the choices less clear cut.

i

DO YOURSELF A FAVOUR

Do something about your financial future, NOW! Learn to save money on your income taxes; how to make informed financial decisions; and how to manage a simple investment programme. A complex and sophisticated financial plan is not necessary. However, it **can** be proven a delay of even one year will cost you a significant amount of money and security at your retirement.

GETTING THE MOST FROM THIS BOOK

This book is meant to be read one chapter a day, taking approximately 15 to 20 minutes per session. Each chapter builds upon the previous one. Upon completion of this book and a certain amount of work on your part, you will have a solid basis for beginning a basic financial plan designed for you, by you. There is an interesting point about making decisions of any kind.   When the plans are not working for you as you want them to, **YOU** can change them and adjust the plan to one that does work for you. By following the chapters in the book, you will learn where you spend your money, what your goals are and what specific steps you can take to improve your financial security.

Start **NOW!** An investment of as little as $50 per month will definitely advance your financial security more than if you put off starting until later.

YOU CAN DO IT!

YOUR COMMITMENT

There is nothing to stop you from reading all the book at one sitting; however, a month's reading and planning is an excellent way to prepare yourself to make the commitment for a lifelong financial plan.

EVERYONE IS WELCOME!

We encourage both men and women to read and enjoy the contents of this book.

THE RIGHT TIME FOR ACTION

Perhaps you are thinking at this point that you are too busy; too involved in other commitments. The time you spend learning the basic financial concepts outlined in this book will improve the quality of your financial life. Store this book where it is easily accessible: your purse, your briefcase, on your kitchen table.

The busy woman may purchase the tapes *FINANCIAL STRATEGIES FOR WOMEN - THE BASICS* (order form in back of book) which discuss some of the main concepts in this book.

Taking **ACTION** is necessary for successful financial management. In order to develop your plan you must realize where you are today and you must determine your future financial needs and goals. This begins with your Net Worth Statement, developed in Chapters 1 to 3.

THE BEST ATTITUDE

Your attitude should be that of a detective whose goal is to find the hidden clues; not to lay blame, put yourself down, or create anxiety because you should/shouldn't have done something.

SEVEN STEPS TO PERSONAL FINANCIAL FREEDOM

1. **Know where you are. Complete your Net Worth Statement and review it at least once a year.**

2. **Define your financial goals based on your personal needs and desires.**

3. **Understand the impact your budget and cash flow have on your financial plans.**

4. **Increase discretionary dollars by decreasing your costs and saving money on expenses.**

5. **Reduce or defer income taxes.**

6. **Increase your knowledge of current financial issues; read, take courses, ask questions and check answers.**

7. **Adjust your goals and plans in accordance with personal changes.**

By the time you complete all the chapters in this book, you will be well on the way to fulfilling all these points. Be sure to complete each exercise as it occurs in the chapter. It will be fun and easy!

Chapter One

HOW TO START PLANNING YOUR FINANCIAL FUTURE

Your financial 'starting block' is your Net Worth. This is the amount by which your assets exceed your liabilities.

ASSETS – LIABILITIES = NET WORTH

ASSETS are possessions which have a resale value. An ASSET would be your home, car, money in the bank, R.R.S.P's., investments in Stocks, Bonds, Mutual Funds, or Guaranteed Investment Certificates (G.I.C.'s), art, gold or gems.

LIABILITIES are financial obligations. A liability may be a mortgage on your home, a loan to purchase an asset such as your car, or any bill .

1

SAMPLE NET WORTH CALCULATION

ASSETS		LIABILITIES	
HOME	$120,000	MORTGAGE	$70,000
CAR	12,000	CAR LOAN	5,000
CASH	1,000	VISA	800
G.I.C.'S.	5,000	GAS CARD	200
R.R.S.P.'S	14,000	AUNT ANN	1,000
TOTAL	**$152,000**	**TOTAL**	**$77,000**

ASSETS	**$152,000**
LIABILITIES	**77,000**
NET WORTH	**$75,000**

BASIC ACCOUNTING PRINCIPLES

Like all accounting, **NET WORTH** is based on certain assumptions. You assume you could sell your assets and obtain the price listed. In actual practice, people under pressure to sell rarely receive their asking price. A **Net Worth Statement** shows whether or not you are achieving an increased Net Worth every year and how much it is increasing, or if not, by how much it is decreasing. If you have a decreasing Net Worth, you are able to identify the problem and act accordingly.

"What do you think Shelley? Will I be able to save if I learn more about managing my money?"

INCREASES AND DECREASES
IN NET WORTH

Example
Decreased net worth can be caused by a drop in the real estate market. You purchased your home two years ago for $140,000 and put $40,000 down. Your home is now worth $120,000. Your mortgage remains close to $100,000 because with the normal amortization of 25 years (the number of years used to calculate the repayment schedule), the first two years pays down little on the principal. Your **Net Worth** has been reduced by approximately $20,000 through no fault of your own.

Conversely, if the Real Estate market goes through a quick increase in prices, your **Net Worth** can increase just as quickly.

OTHER ASSETS

Additional assets include things like one half of your spouse's pension plan upon dissolution of a marriage, or one half the value of a business owned by you and a partner. Think about additional items which are part of your Net Worth. Jewellery, Antiques, Stocks or Bonds, (check their value with a Broker or Financial Consultant) and Insurance Policies that have a cash value (check with your Insurance Agent) may be included.

Read any documents you think may have some impact on your future finances. Assets, such as higher education or specific skills, do not contribute to your Net Worth in dollars but are certainly valuable.

Chapters 2 and 3 have details on listing your Assets and Liabilities. Once you have read them, complete the **Net Worth Statement** in the back of this book.

Make a photocopy of the form before you use it and you will be able to do a **Net Worth Statement** whenever you wish to check your progress.

Once you know your present **Net Worth**, the question is how to increase it. You start by finding out where your money is being spent each month. (The Budget, Chapter 4.)

NOTE:

W.I.N. will send you an evaluation of your Net Worth as part of their commitment to helping women with their financial security. Send the completed "Personal Financial Review" located in the back of this book to:

> **W.I.N. (Women's Investment Network) Inc.**
> **981 Wellington Rd. South, Suite 402**
> **London, Ontario**
> **N6E 3A9**

In order to provide a sound evaluation, we require you to include your age, profession and phone number. Please include a stamped, self-addressed 9" x 12" envelope. All information will be handled by a professional Financial Consultant and kept confidential.

Chapter Two

ASSETS

"Diamonds are a girl's best friend"
ANON.

Assets are items you own or partly own which increase your Net Worth. Your home, cottage, and car are assets. Yes, even your diamonds are assets. Your mortgage or loans against these assets are liabilities and decrease the net value of your assets.

ASSETS INCLUDE:
- Money in any bank account
- Guaranteed Investment Certificates
- Government Treasury Bills
- Money Market accounts
- Term Deposits, plus unpaid interest
- Canada Savings Bonds, plus unpaid interest
- Mutual Funds
- Stocks
- Bonds
- Life Insurance Policy Cash Value

YOUR HOME AS AN ASSET

For example, you have owned your home for ten years and you paid $130,000 for it. You must have it appraised for the approximate value before putting it in your Net Worth Statement. A look at comparable homes in your neighbourhood shows you they are selling for $140,000 - $145,000. These homes must have the same attributes as yours (garage, air conditioning, wall to wall carpeting, etc.). You can ask for a free evaluation from a Real Estate Broker or Representative. They will then check all the comparable homes in your area and compare the selling prices to your home.

Remember, your home is only worth this value if it actually sells for $140,000 to $145,000.

LIQUIDITY

Some assets are more liquid than others. Liquid assets include cash in the bank, cashable bonds such as Canada Savings Bonds or Money Market Mutual Funds. An asset loses its liquidity when you would have difficulty obtaining cash quickly in case of emergency or necessity.

YOUR CAR AS AN ASSET

Your vehicle is an asset which may be difficult to evaluate. The 'Red Book or Blue Book' values quote predetermined wholesale or retail values for all used vehicles sold in Canada. What you would actually receive if you needed to sell your vehicle is an entirely different story.

WHEN AN ASSET IS NOT AN ASSET!

Sometimes you think your car is an asset but, if you owe more on it than it's worth, it is not an asset but a liability.

This is a depressing situation and it is one that you should consider when purchasing. This situation may occur when you put little or nothing down and spread your payments over a long time – four or five years. High mileage or poor maintenance are contributing factors since they both lower the price someone will pay when you want to sell your car.

THE VALUE OF YOUR SHARES OR UNITS

You can look up the Net Asset Value Per Share of Mutual Funds or Stocks in your local newspaper, the Financial Post, the Financial Times or the Globe and Mail. Ask your Insurance Agent for the Cash Values in Whole Life Insurance Policies, especially if you have had them for a long period of time.

ACCURATE APPRAISAL OF YOUR ASSETS

You can be accurate when assessing your money assets at a particular time. However, you may not be able to sell them at a moment's notice if you need cash. G.I.C.'S and Term deposits have terms and usually you can't cash them before the term is over. If you can cash them, you often receive a reduction in the amount of interest you receive as a penalty. Sometimes you are not permitted to cash in these investments for any reason.

A COLLATERAL LOAN

The Financial Institution may offer you a loan (a liability) while holding some of your investments as security (collateral). Therefore, your asset is actually reduced by the amount of the loan.

Example
You invested $10,000 in a five year term deposit paying 10% yearly. Two years later the bank lends you $5,000 at 12% and holds your term deposit as collateral. The loan must be repaid before you could cash your investment. You do not have access to the other $5,000 of your term deposit or any of the interest.

PLANNING TIP

Divide your $10,000 investment into two or more separate investments for more flexibility. Be sure this does not reduce your interest rate.

OTHER ASSETS

Paintings, antiques, collections, jewellery or any other items which have value are assets. Two difficulties arise. It is often difficult to put an accurate value on these items and if you ever needed to sell them to realize their 'cash value', you probably would not receive their true or appraised worth.

Remember the antique toy mania. People were paying thousands of dollars for 'old toys'. The bottom dropped out and the value was gone. This also happened with many other 'hot' collections.

The real value of something is what someone will pay **at the time** you want or need to sell the item.

ASSETS NOT USUALLY COUNTED

Assets not usually counted in your Net Worth are furniture and household possessions. Their value is decreased the moment the transaction took place. For example, if you **had** to sell your furniture, you would receive much less than what you paid, even if you sold it immediately after purchase.

A sofa suite that cost $1,000, may only sell for $300 - $400 second hand. People tend to want real 'bargains' when they buy second hand furniture.

SPECIAL OCCASION WARDROBE

Some fur coats and evening gowns have a significantly lower value and are not usually counted in your assets. Diamond engagement rings have a reduced value, but are still assets.

> ACTION PLAN: Complete the Asset side of your Personal Financial Review in the back of the book.

"I wonder if I can count my old engagement ring as an asset?"

Chapter Three

LIABILITIES

Liabilities are amounts of money or a debt you owe.

Liabilities are:

- Mortgage
- Car loans
- Credit Cards
- Overdue bills
- Other Loans
    - Consolidation Loans
    - Loans (with assets as collateral)
    - Store accounts
    - Finance company loans
    - Amounts owing to friends

HOW DEBT AFFECTS YOU

Debt is enough of a problem by itself but some debts have a greater effect on your life. Loans can be at a low or high interest rate. The higher the interest rate the more you pay back before the principal is paid.

Example

You obtain a loan from a relative as a favour to buy a new refrigerator. You agree to pay only the interest for one year at 5%. On a loan of $1,000 held for one full year, the interest is $50.

Buy the refrigerator for $1,000 on a store credit card and keep the amount the same for one year and the interest paid by you would be $288 at 2.4% per month. Over five and a half times the amount you paid your relative!

WHERE TO FIND INFORMATION

Credit cards all have pertinent information on the back of the statement. It is sometimes easy to overlook because the monthly amount is often 2.4% but this translates into 28.8% per year.

KNOW YOUR CREDIT CONTRACTS

Read the contract on the back of the statements. You need to know the interest rate charged and the due date of the payments because you will want to pay off the accounts with the highest interest rate first. Of course, it is always better if you paid off all your accounts completely but, if you pay down or charge less on the highest interest rate accounts, you can save money on credit charges.

CONSOLIDATION LOANS

Consolidation loans should be considered when you need to gather all debts into one and have to pay only one amount. This is usually lower than the total of the previous accounts and interest payments. Shop until you find the lowest interest rate. You should be able to obtain your loan at a Financial Institution with lower rates, rather than at stores or on credit cards with high interest charges.

It is a challenge NOT to charge on the other accounts now that they have zero balances. Put them away if overspending has been a problem.

RAPID PAYMENT PLAN

Plan to pay the consolidation loan in as short a period as possible. When the repayment period is lengthened, it costs you as much or more than you would have paid since you are repaying the principal at a slower rate and therefore paying the interest for a longer period. Check the terms of the loan and be sure you can pay down additional amounts when you are able. Credit grantors may not allow you to pay off additional amounts or to pay off the loan entirely before the end of the terms, or they may charge you a penalty for doing so.

Ask questions. Know the facts. Make decisions and realize the results of your choices.

"When is borrowing a smart move?"

GETTING THE MOST FROM YOUR CREDIT CARDS

Use the credit cards and store cards as charge cards and pay them off every month. You have convenience and you pay no interest. You may save bank charges because you pay with one cheque instead of several. The challenge is not to let your charges go past the monthly payment period or let them 'pile up'. Your balance would increase and the interest payment would start.

HOW CREDIT HELPS

Credit is a very important part of our lives. It can save us great amounts of money or cost us even greater amounts.

When you find a real bargain, or interest rates are very low, borrowing to purchase may be a wise move. However you need to be sure the item is needed and you do not charge something you would **NOT** have purchased if you had to spend actual dollars.

WHEN DOES IT MAKE GOOD SENSE TO BORROW?

When should you borrow? No one can tell anyone else when to borrow. However, most of us would not be able to buy a home without borrowing (mortgaging) for our home. Many also would not be able to buy a vehicle without a loan. (See the Chapter 15 on car purchases for the exact results of this action.)

There are times when borrowing makes sense. If you are in a high tax bracket (earning over $50,000 in taxable income) borrowing to contribute to your R.R.S.P. is beneficial. Repay the money in one year or less, and you save 50% on your income tax, minus the interest rate on the loan. Even though the interest is not a tax deduction, the numbers still support this plan.

This programme is one that should be discussed with a qualified Financial Consultant. It is important you qualify for the loan, understand the total programme, are comfortable with the risk involved and are in a high tax bracket.

LEVERAGE PROGRAMMES

Currently, you can also still deduct the interest you paid on money borrowed to invest (See Chapter 21 on Leveraging) in Equities such as Stocks, Mutual Funds or Canadian companies. You should discuss this with your Professional Financial Planner. Choose someone you can trust in dealing with your monies.

> ACTION PLAN: Complete the Liability Section of the Personal Financial Review located in the back of this book. Calculate your personal Net Worth. We recommend you repeat this exercise on a regular basis.

Chapter
Four

THE BUDGET

BUDGET... DIET... Two words that strike fear in the hearts of most women. Both are misunderstood. If you eat, you have a diet. If you have an income from any source and you spend some or all of it, you have a budget. The fear comes from thinking these concepts are stricter than they really need to be.

Before you make changes, you need to know where your money is going. Know your spending habits. Write down all your expenses for one month in a note book. Or, keep all the cash register receipts and simply write the items on the back. Start today! In one month you will have all the information you need to analyze where and how you spend your money.

FIXED EXPENSES

Rent, mortgage payments, car or loan payments, insurance costs and utilities are difficult to change quickly. These are considered fixed expenses.

15

VARIABLE EXPENSES

Variable expenses are those which generally move up and down from one month to the next. Groceries, gas and maintenance for your car, the long distance phone bill and personal care costs, are some variable expenses. Usually, these items can be reduced fairly quickly and easily.

IRREGULAR EXPENSES

Irregular expenses come due either once a year, or every 2, 3, or 6 months. Sometimes these 'occasional' payments may disrupt your budget. Life insurance, house/car insurance, property or income taxes, car or driver's license are examples of irregular expenses. These expenses should be included in your budget.

SAMPLE BUDGET

- Shelter
- Food
- Transportation
- Clothing
- Recreation
- Entertainment
- Savings
- Personal care
- Telephone
- Utilities
- Vacation
- **MISCELLANEOUS**

MINIMIZE MISCELLANEOUS

The miscellaneous category is a 'catch all' that should be kept to a minimum. The purpose of a budget is to analyze where you are spending your money and identify where you can cut back or change.

Almost every item which lands in the miscellaneous category can be placed in one of the other columns. Snack food and restaurant meals should be in *FOOD*, unless you are trying to identify how much money you are spending by eating out .

Each category may be divided into subsections for this purpose. For example, *SHELTER* can include mortgage payment, property taxes, utilities (gas, electric, water, sewer) and Home/Condominium or Tenants Insurance.

THE QUICK METHOD

If using the cashier receipt method, once a week take the receipts out of your wallet and sort them into envelopes each marked with the category or transfer the amounts directly to your notebook. If one or two slipped in without notations, you can probably remember what they were. Leaving them all until the end of the month gives you a task bigger than you may want to tackle, causing you to feel defeated before you begin!

WHERE DO YOU WANT TO SPEND YOUR MONEY?

After you know where you really spend your money, the next step is to decide where you **want** to spend your dollars. The fixed expenses can't be changed unless you make lifestyle changes. Variable expenses may be reduced more quickly; allowing you to make significant changes.

One woman identified her grocery expenses were increased over 100% due to her eating out at lunch and quick 'after work' meals. She solved this by taking a bag lunch and starting her evening meal preparations during her breakfast so supper was almost ready upon her arrival home. She also found these meals more nutritious and less fattening – a double benefit!

BUDGETING HELPS!

Budget is really DECIDING where you want to spend your dollars so you do not let money slip away without making definite decisions.

DISCRETIONARY SPENDING

Discretionary dollars are those not required for your daily living **needs**. Your goals show you where these dollars should be spent.

PAY YOURSELF FIRST

In most budget samples, saving is the last item. Put savings first for a dramatic improvement in your finances. Calculate your total income, take 10% (more if possible) and put that amount at the top of the budget sheet; deduct this from your income and use the balance for your expenses. Several chapters are devoted to savings and investing. In the meantime, deposit this amount in a separate savings account.

KEEPING FLEXIBLE

A crisis situation such as being laid off or a family emergency can cause a budget to go 'out the window' Savings provide the cushion needed to take the stress out of this situation.

Remember, **KNOWLEDGE IS POWER** and if you know what you spend and why, you are in charge of your budget and can change it.

You run the budget, it does not run you.

There are only two things you can do when expenses exceed income; increase your income or decrease your expenses. You can increase your income by finding a higher paying job, negotiating a raise or getting a second job. You decrease your expenses by reducing or eliminating expenses which do not really add to the quality of your life. Sometimes you must do both.

**If everyone learned this concept,
there would be no 'deficit'.**

ACTION PLAN: Complete the Income and Expenses portion of the Budget at the back of this book. Make copies before you complete your entries so you will be able to repeat this exercise when your expenses or income change.

Chapter

Five

BANKING AND YOU

TYPES OF ACCOUNTS

In the past, there were only three types of accounts: Savings, Chequing and Current (used for business). Now there are many variations of accounts, charges and interest rates at each different Bank, Trust Company, or Credit Union.

You need at least two or perhaps three accounts at a Financial Institution to handle your money easily.

1. Set up a regular **Savings Account** to deposit a monthly amount for short term savings. This will provide available money for irregular expenses such as yearly insurance payments, holiday and birthday presents, reserves for car repairs and vacations. The account may allow you to write a few free cheques each month. Know how many cheques you are able to write free, since additional cheques often cost more per cheque than a chequing account.

2. **High Interest or Treasury Bill Accounts** pay a higher interest rate than the regular savings account. Depending on the balance, a certain number of cheques may be written free each month. These accounts often need a balance of $3,000 to $5,000 before the higher interest rate applies. Be sure you know what that amount is because even one dollar less than the required sum will negate the higher interest.

   When you have a consistently high balance in a high interest account, you should explore other options which may increase the returns, give you tax savings or both.

3. **Chequing Accounts** allow you to pay only for those cheques which are deducted from your account each month, or a level monthly charge. If you do not write a lot of cheques, the 'pay as you go' type is best.

   If you write a large number of cheques, the level monthly charge account gives you additional services such as free cheques, free money orders and a limit on monthly charges, no matter how many cheques you write each month. Be sure you regularly write more cheques a month than the basic charge would cover.

Example
If $.50 is charged for each cheque, you need to write more than 12 cheques per month before you save on a $5.95 flat fee account. Other services are often included which may be important to you.

---

4. A combination of these accounts is a **Chequing/ Savings Account**. When you keep a solid balance of $1,000 in your account, you may write any number of cheques without paying any charges. You will be charged for all the month's cheques if the balance drops below the minimum anytime during the month.

SAFETY DEPOSIT BOXES

Safety Deposit Boxes are an excellent place to keep valuables such as documents and jewellery. Keep originals of wills, marriage certificate, birth certificate, passport or other important documents in your Safety Deposit Box. You may deduct the cost of the Safety Deposit box as a banking charge on your income tax when you store assets or investments in it. Keep your key in a safe place.

PAYING BILLS

Many utility bills, your municipal tax bill and several other bills, may be paid at Financial Institutions. The charge is included in level charge accounts. The convenience may make the level fee account worth the cost.

MISTAKES IN YOUR ACCOUNT

If there are errors or withdrawals from your account which you do not understand, question the teller or manager. If there is an error, the entry can be reversed. Always check that the entries in your passbook agree with those from your cheque register. When you pay your bills, write the cheque number both in your cheque register and on the bill. These records are invaluable if discrepancies occur in any of your accounts.

POINTS TO REMEMBER

1. Keep track of your cheques. It costs between $10 and $20 for each N.S.F. cheque. Do not overdraw your account as you will be charged a higher interest rate for overdraft charges. You can set up agreements at your Bank or Trust Company between your accounts, so if a cheque is presented which cannot be covered with the present balance in your chequing account, the appropriate amount will be transferred from your other account(s) to cover the overdraft. There is usually a minimal charge for this service.

2. If part of your financial strategy is to keep some of your money accessible, compare the current interest rates from several banks. You might as well have the best interest rate.

3. You need to have a bank card for convenience. The Personal Identification Number (P.I.N.) provides easy access to your account through banking machines so you may deposit and withdraw money. You are charged a service charge on Interac machines but no service charge when you use your own bank machines.

4. Introduce yourself to your Bank Manager. When an emergency strikes, you know someone to call. They will be able to help you with loans and other services.

5. If you visit the United States often, you should have a U.S. Account. When you transfer from a Canadian Account to an American Account, you will receive a better rate on converting your Canadian money. It is only 1/2 to 3/4 %, and on $20 it doesn't make much difference. On $2,000 the difference could buy you lunch!

Chapter Six

SAVING

CREATE THE HABIT

Saving for any reason is an excellent habit. You need to save for a variety of reasons; to create a cash cushion; to buy things you don't want to charge; to save for the future, for a home, retirement or for your children's education.

It is interesting, when putting a budget together, savings tends to be the last on the list. Many people have the misconception that:

SAVINGS = WHAT IS "LEFT OVER"

WHERE TO PUT SAVINGS IN YOUR BUDGET

When **you put savings first** every pay, you take what is left to pay the bills and costs of living.

PAYROLL DEDUCTION PLAN

The easiest way to save is involvement in some type of payroll deduction plan. You save before you see the money. Many companies have such plans and some even match the employee's share with their own contribution, up to a specific amount or percentage. Sometimes, the money must remain in the account for a specified time or withdrawn for specific reasons such as mortgage pay down or on a specific date. Use these plans to attain your goals.

A SECURE WAY TO START

Canada Savings Bonds are a sound way to start your regular savings plan. You save, and if there is a real emergency, the money is easily accessible. Remember interest is only paid for completed months.

USING MONTHLY MUTUAL FUND (P.A.C.) ACCOUNTS

Regular contributions to a Savings Account or into a monthly Mutual Fund Account can be deducted through a Pre-Authorized Cheque Plan (P.A.C.) from your bank account. This could accomplish your goal for easily accessible money and regular savings at the same time.

FIVE KEYS TO A SOLID
SAVINGS HABIT

1. Make regular payments every pay or every other pay.

2. Achieve a solid cash cushion for emergencies which is easily accessible.

3. Obtain the best interest rate possible.

4. Leave some room in your budget for small emergencies or an increase in daily living costs. You don't want to break the habit for small things.

5. Set up your Registered Retirement Savings Plan (R.R.S.P.'S.) on a monthly basis, or use a designated Savings Account.

Set up separate accounts for each type of savings. Have a definite amount you save each year. These savings amounts go right to the Asset or plus side of your Net Worth Statement.

It makes you feel great to take charge of your financial welfare.

YOUR HOME AS AN ASSET

In the past, many people have used their home to increase their Net Worth. This works well when the value of homes are increasing at a rate faster than the rate of inflation. Sometimes, values decrease as in the most recent recession.

You should think of your home NOT as a savings plan but as shelter. If the resale value has increased when it is time to sell, it becomes an added benefit to you.

THE 'RIGHT' AMOUNT

The usual 'rule of thumb' for savings is **10%** of your income.

The more you save earlier in your life, the more it will be worth later (as long as you don't touch it.) One dollar ($1.00) invested at 5% when you are 20 will be worth $8.98 when you are 65.

INCREASE YOUR RETURNS QUICKLY

Two things contribute to how your money grows:
            Rate of Return and *Time*.
Increase either, Rate of Return or Time, and you add considerable dollars to your asset base. Increase both for truly spectacular results.

RATE OF RETURN

The amount of increase of your investment divided by the number of years you have held the investment is known as the *Rate of Return*.

1. **Interest** from a Bank, Trust Company or Credit Union, Money Market Mutual Funds, Canada Savings Bonds, or Term deposits is usually predetermined and paid at regular intervals, e.g. monthly, yearly.

2. **Dividends** are the returns created by owning shares of a company and receiving a share of their profits.

3. **Capital Gains** are the increase of the value of property that you own (which could be the shares of a company, rental property, or fine art).

HOW TO CALCULATE
YOUR RATE OF RETURN

Calculate the Rate of Return by subtracting the amount of your original investment (include any capital expenditures) from the current value of the property, shares or item; then divide by the number of years you have owned the item. This is your Rate of Return.

COMPOUNDING:
MAKING TIME WORK FOR YOU

Time improves the value of your investments in increasing increments because of **compounding**. You get a 10% return on your investment of $100, which is $10 for one year. In year two, you receive the 10% return on the original investment plus on the $10 interest you earned in the first year. Your interest for the second year is $11. The third year at 10% you receive interest on the $121 which is $12.10.

COMPOUNDING PAYS

You should make sure that your interest investments are all compounded and the interest stays within the investment to gain further interest. When you take the returns out of the investment and perhaps spend it, you are taking away one of the very best ways to increase your Net Worth.

SPEED UP COMPOUNDING

The more often compounding occurs, the faster your Rate of Return increases. For instance, on your $100 if you receive 10% interest, compounded annually, your investment would be worth $672.75 after 20 years. If the same $100 at 10% per year, compounded monthly (.833% per month) you would have $732.23 or more than $59 at the end of 20 years.

WHAT DIFFERENCE DOES ONE PERCENT MAKE?

Take $100 and invest it for 20 years at 10% compounded annually and the result is $673. If you found an investment which paid 11% for 20 years you would have $806 or an increase of $133. Not bad for a 1% increase!

Have some fun! Try calculating how much difference it would make if you could obtain that 1% more return **AND** compound your investment on a monthly basis. Only one hundred dollars at 11% compounded monthly would be over $893 in 20 years.

ANOTHER WAY TO MAXIMIZE YOUR INVESTMENT

What would happen if you contributed **$100 EACH MONTH** to a plan which returned you an average of 10% per year compounded monthly? You would have about $75,165 in 20 years. Increase the return on your investment to 12% and you would have over $98,925. That's great!

THE RULE OF 72

A quick way to calculate how often your money will double in value is to use the rule of 72. You divide 72 by the yearly percentage received on your investment. This is the amount of time it will take you to double your money. If your investment earns a 7.2% rate of return per year, it will take 10 years for your money to double. If you could make your investment return 14.4% per year, it would only take five years to double your original investment. This is a 'rule of thumb' and should only be used as a quick calculation.

CHART:

Interest rate	5%	7.2%	10%	12%	15%	18%
Years to double	14.4	10	7.2	6	4.8	4

Chapter
Seven

GOALS FOR SAVINGS

SHORT TERM SAVINGS

Goals and needs up to two years are considered short term savings. You need enough cash on hand to cover emergencies, unemployment for up to three months, vacations and purchases too large to be saved for over a couple of pay cheques. Short term savings may also be a down payment on a home when you are able to accumulate it within two years.

Saving the emergency fund is a challenge at first especially when you are young or starting over. It is better to set aside the same amount each month, even if you have to 'dip' into it occasionally. Irregular deposits seldom work. It is too easy to put off starting until next month.

Pay cash for your purchases. It is amazing how it is easier to say "no" to impulse purchases when you only have $20 in your purse than if you are just 'pulling out the credit card'. Save the plastic for those emergencies which always seem to crop up when you least expect them.

ESTIMATING HOW MUCH YOU SHOULD HAVE IN YOUR SHORT TERM ACCOUNT

If you are earning $20,000 a year, you would need $5,000 to $10,000 for three to six months emergency expenses. Deposit this amount in a High Interest or Money Market Mutual Fund Account for ease of withdrawal and flexibility. This sounds like a lot of money and you are right! Remember, you don't take home all the money you earn. At $20,000 a year, your take home pay would be around $300 per week. Now you are aiming at between $3,900 and $7,800 for your 'fund'. You could also deduct work related expenses such as travel, lunches, accessories, and dry cleaning bills from this amount. Perhaps $3,000 (the three month target) to $5,000 (the six month target) would be sufficient to handle your expenses.

JOB SEARCH EXPENSES

You must include some money to cover the costs of looking for a job. Depending on the type of position you are seeking, looking for a job can be fairly expensive.

Keeping your credit purchases down will also help you manage when you are unemployed or sick for a short time. When something happens, cut your spending to the minimum and **try not to charge anything.**

MY SHORT TERM SAVINGS GOALS

DAILY INTEREST SAVINGS	$ _____
CANADA SAVINGS BONDS	$ _____
MONEY MARKET FUND	$ _____
SEPARATE SAVINGS	$ _____
TOTAL	$ _____

MEDIUM TERM SAVINGS

Medium term savings could be for as short a time as three years or as long as 10 to 15 years, depending on how long you will be earning money before you retire.

Medium term savings for most people include educational plans for their children or themselves. (Refer to Chapter 26, Saving for Education for more detailed information.)

When you are young and starting to earn a living, medium term savings goals could include the down payment for your home.

Medium term savings goals may also include retirement plans especially when you are over age 50.

PLANNING AHEAD

Often it is difficult to look forward ten years. When your income barely stretches to cover daily expenses, you may wonder why you are spending time thinking about what you want ten or more years from now. If you do not start thinking about what lifestyle you would like, you will never have it. You will never put the plans in place which will allow you to prepare financially, and without financial preparation many retirement lifestyles will not be possible.

Financial Consultants hear the lament, "I wish I had known what I know now, back when I was twenty."OR "If I had only put a little away from the time I started working, I would be rich today!" more often than any other comment.

"Everyone needs a vacation, don't they?"

ASK SOMEONE WHO HAS
ACHIEVED WHAT YOU WANT!

Ask some people you think are financially secure how they achieved this. One of the most common themes you will hear is they knew what they wanted and made the commitment to putting time, effort and money into this endeavour.

Knowing what you want is one key. Another key is making the commitment and following through.

TEN YEAR GOALS	I WILL NEED
1. _____	$ _____
2. _____	$ _____
3. _____	$ _____
4. _____	$ _____
TOTAL	$ _____

LONG TERM SAVINGS

Long term savings continues for over 10 or 15 years or longer, based on your present age.

WHEN SHOULD YOU START TO SAVE FOR LONG TERM?

Young people look at retirement as 'long term', and often do not give any thought to this long term need. As you get older, you may have trouble 'getting around' to actually planning for your retirement.

IS IT TOO LATE TO START SAVING?

People in their thirties and forties are still able to make regular contributions and have significant amounts of money available for their retirement. However, as you get closer to retirement age, it takes larger contributions to achieve significant retirement funds since money is working for a shorter period of time; compounding for fewer years and therefore, giving you less money at retirement.

REASONS FOR LONG TERM SAVINGS

Some people spend their lives working for a company while their goal is to change their lifestyle in a significant way. Usually this action requires a large amount of money. Other people think the ultimate career choice is to go into business for themselves. They need a hefty amount of money for start up costs, operating expenses and their personal living expenses.

Exotic or extended vacations or a vacation home are often long term savings goals.

Although retirement is the most usual long term goal, anything for which you put away some money over a ten year span or more, is considered to be long term.

WRITTEN GOALS ARE MORE ATTAINABLE

As in all your financial plans, you should write down your goals. You may change them as time goes by, if your personal needs and goals change. If your ideas or goals change, you will at least have some money already committed. Once again, you make the plans, so you are the one who decides to change them.

LONG TERM GOALS	I WILL NEED
1. _____	$ _____
2. _____	$ _____
3. _____	$ _____
4. _____	$ _____
TOTAL	$ _____

"I work hard for my money. I deserve to pay myself first."

Chapter Eight

INVESTING

Most people never start to invest. Savings is where everyone starts and many people finish. If you have no savings you will have no investments. A savings plan is where you take a regular amount each month and deposit it into a special account which you do not touch. The purpose is to keep some short term money handy for the times when the unexpected happens. Investing is for the long term, where you use a plan which includes more aggressive strategies.

Investing requires diversification from interest bearing debt investments into Mutual Funds or Stocks, which give you a return in Dividends or Capital Gains. (See Chapter 21 for how these investments are taxed).

CAPITAL GAIN OR LOSS

Capital Gain is when you sell your shares for more than what they cost. On a Capital Loss you sell for less than you paid per share.

STOCKS

One easy way to buy part of a company is to purchase shares from a Stock Broker. You can buy Stock in a company directly, or shares of a company listed on the Stock Exchange. Some small companies ask their friends and relatives to purchase shares and they will share their profits with you. You must ask yourself, "Do I know enough about this company, its management, its marketing and feasibility to make an informed decision?".

MUTUAL FUNDS

Mutual Funds are a collection of shares in many companies. Equity Mutual Funds are those which invest across many sectors in the economy in companies large or small. Bond Funds buy and sell mostly Bonds. Money Market Mutual Funds use Treasury Bills to increase the interest they earn. Balanced Funds use varying combinations of these investments to take advantage of market fluctuations in Stocks, Bonds and Interest. The investments are chosen by Professional Money Managers who use a variety of methods to choose Shares of companies which produce good profits, Bonds which produce the highest return or short term/long term Interest investments which produce the highest return.

The benefit of a Mutual Fund is, you have a selection of different companies in your portfolio so you achieve instant diversification, professional management and are sent statements which give all the information needed for your income tax returns.

TYPES OF INVESTMENTS

Interest Bearing Accounts are usually open (you can take your money out at any time) and have a very low interest rate which fluctuates with the prime rate.

Guaranteed Investment Certificates (G.I.C.'s) are usually 'locked in' for a specific period of time, usually one to five years at a set rate of interest. When interest rates are low, use the shorter term of one or two years. When interest rates are high, invest for the longer terms with at least part of your portfolio.

Money Market Accounts are based on the 90 day Treasury Bill interest rate and are higher than simple interest bearing accounts, but lower than the guaranteed investment certificate rate as a rule. These accounts are accessible and not 'locked in'.

Insurance Policy Plans are invested with the Insurance Company in term deposits (G.I.C.'S) or Segregated Funds. Segregated Funds are monies kept separate from the Insurance Company's other money. These funds are usually creditor proof.

Mutual Funds come in several forms such as Equity, Balanced, Bond, Asset Allocation, Dividend, Mortgage and Real Estate funds, and any combination of these. The prospectus will tell you whether or not a fund qualifies for R.R.S.P.'S. If you are using a Self Directed Plan, you are also allowed to include up to 20% of Foreign Mutual Funds.

Bonds are long term debt sold by companies, utilities and governments (local, provincial, and federal) which yield a prescribed rate of interest until maturity. When a Bond pays higher interest than you can get currently for a debt instrument, it sells for a premium which results in a higher return. If a Bond pays lower interest than you can obtain currently, they are discounted and your return is lower. They may be added to your R.R.S.P. if they are Canadian or within the foreign content guidelines.

Stocks are shares of a company which pay Dividends or have an increase in value which is a Capital Gain. Many Stocks are listed on the major stock exchanges in Canada and are eligible for your R.R.S.P. There are special regulations for Stocks in companies which are not listed on the Stock Exchanges in Canada.

RISK

How do you define risk when you are talking about investing? Some people think it is risky to do anything and therefore do nothing. Others never think of the risk or don't ask questions to determine risk. There is more risk in doing nothing than putting together a diverse and intelligent financial plan.

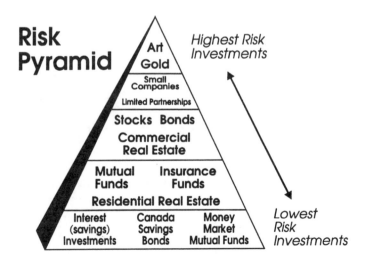

Ask your Financial Consultant about the benefits of either Stocks or Mutual Funds. The return on the investment is often projected over a five, ten year or longer period. If the Stock Market decreases and you decide to sell, you may lose money. This is one of the reasons why many consultants project returns over a five or ten year period of time.

THE DOUBLE BENEFIT

When you buy Shares in companies or Mutual Funds, you double the benefit. You receive Dividends on a more or less regular basis and when you sell the Shares, you hopefully receive a Capital Gain because you sold them for more than what you paid per share.

When you invest in Mutual Funds, the Professional Manager buys and sells continuously so there are 'realized' Capital Gains or Losses during any one year. Both Dividends and Capital Gains are taxed less than an investment which pays Interest.

**START SAVING NOW,
PAY YOURSELF 10% FIRST**

ACTION PLAN: Continually learn about new investments and strategies. Take advantage of all income tax breaks for investments.

WHERE TO START WITH
YOUR MONEY PLANS

1. Become debt free, treat your credit cards as monthly bills.

2. Protect your risks by knowing what they are, what the chances are of each risk occurring, and have only the appropriate insurance.

3. State and follow your short term savings goals.

4. Include money for the education of your children or yourself.

5. Know how much you will require for basic needs at retirement and how you plan to achieve your goal.

6. Diversify your investments. Do not have only one type of investment such as Interest. Know and use other types.

7. Obtain professional assistance, but understand at all times exactly what your investments are, what the returns are and the type of return you can expect.

8. Remember you may begin a monthly plan for as little as $50 by buying a portfolio of Stocks in the Mutual Fund of your choice.

DO NOT ALLOW ANYONE ACCESS TO YOUR ACCOUNTS OR FOLLOW ANYONE'S ADVICE WITHOUT UNDERSTANDING IT.

YOU ARE RESPONSIBLE FOR YOUR MONEY!

Chapter Nine

MAKING MONEY GROW

The start of your financial plan is knowing where you are. This consists of your list of assets and liabilities which translates into your Net Worth Statement. The budget or cash flow consists of your monthly (yearly) income and expenses. The earlier chapters are designed so you will know what you have and what you spend. In future chapters you will learn some ways to save on your regular and irregular expenses, which if properly used, will result in an increased Net Worth.

Now that you know where you are, you must start to plan where you want to be at some future time. Usually we think of a secure retirement as a goal. Your goals, however, may be an education for your children or yourself (see Chapter 26 on Saving for Education), to own your first home or a larger home in a better location. Whatever your present goals are, you need to plan for them. Planning includes a factor for emergencies, and sometimes emergencies make you totally readjust your plans. If you have a plan, you can change it.

If you have no plan, you can not change it and you usually go along spending money and as a result, can get deep in debt quickly. The important point is to start NOW! If you delay your plan by only one year, you lose hundreds of thousands of dollars.

Example I
If you are 20 years old and start a $100 a month plan into a Mutual Fund which averages 12% per year until you are 65, you will have approximately $2,145,000.

If you waited only **ONE YEAR** until you were 21 years old to start this plan, you would have only $1,902,000 or **$242,000 less! That is almost a quarter of a million dollars.** Could you use a quarter of a million dollars at age 65? **Probably!**

Example II
If you are 40 years old and start your plan at $250 per month into the same mutual fund(s) averaging 12% per year until you are 65, you will have approximately $469,700. Put off starting for only one year and you would have about $414,000 or **$55,700** less!

Both examples are based on monthly purchase plans of Mutual Funds since this is a simple way to begin your regular saving and investing habits. Since Mutual Funds are a logical investment for at least a portion of anyone's plan, it is important to understand what a Mutual Fund is and how it would work for you.

MUTUAL FUNDS

A Mutual Fund is a pool of money (Capital) deposited by many investors. This pool of money is handled by a professional manager or management company both for the administration of these funds and the investments.

A portfolio manager decides when to buy and sell the investments in the portfolio in keeping with the objectives of the fund. Every fund must have a prospectus on file with the Security Commission of the province where it is sold. The prospectus states the goals and objectives of the fund, the officers of the management company, the fees and any restrictions. A management company usually directs several funds with different focuses, strategies and goals. One goal always is to increase the profits so the investment will increase in value. A fund sells **shares** or **units** depending on how the fund is registered.

WHAT YOU OWN

Each shareholder or unitholder owns a percentage of the total holdings of the fund. A fund may be open or closed. An **open fund** is allowed to have an unlimited number of investors. No matter how large the number of people who want to invest, your investment must be accepted. It is the portfolio manager's job to invest this money in ways which help the fund achieve its goals.

A **closed fund** has a specific number of shares or a specific amount of money under administration. A person may not buy a share unless someone else is willing to sell their share. If you own shares and wish to sell, you must find someone willing to buy. The result is a certain amount of inflexibility with this type of fund.

THE PROSPECTUS

The **prospectus** states the objectives of the Fund, management fees, regulations for changing focus or any rules and other information pertinent to the fund. It also states whether or not the fund is eligible for your R.R.S.P. A fund must keep the non Canadian component to less than 20% to be eligible. Funds not eligible for an R.R.S.P. may have unlimited international investments as long as the investments fit the goals of the fund.

An **annual report** and **quarterly reports** show the shares of companies currently owned by the Fund, total assets, the money held as cash and other important information.

WHY MUTUAL FUNDS

Mutual Funds are extremely popular for the small investor since a plan can be:

1. For a small or large amount.

2. Regular payments on a pre authorized cheque (P.A.C.) plan and the option of adding lump sums at any time.

3. Immediate investment in a number of companies or bonds.

4. Withdrawal of any portion on short notice except in a real estate fund or a closed fund.

5. The Net Asset Value per share is printed in the financial newspapers and many daily newspapers. Take this amount and multiply it by the number of shares you own for the value of your investment as of the previous day.

INCOME OR GROWTH

Funds fall into two categories when analyzing their returns. They are either income funds or growth funds.

Income Funds invest mainly in bonds, mortgages, preferred shares, money market funds or a combination of these.

Growth Funds are mainly invested in equity stocks and may be focused across the stock market or a specific sector. Funds which are focused on a sector such as precious metals or natural resources are called Specialty Funds.

Specialty Funds are considered to be more volatile than broader based, diversified funds. **Balanced Funds** use a combination of both income and growth investments.

COMMISSIONS

The cost to purchase funds is called a 'load'. There are **front end load funds, deferred sales charge funds** and **no load funds**. The maximum load or commission and how it may be charged is stated in the prospectus. All commissions or load on front end load funds are currently negotiable.

Front end sales charges are deducted from the original investment with the remainder of the money invested in the fund.

Deferred sales charge funds take from five to nine years before they are completely free from commission upon withdrawal. These funds are appropriate for monies you will not require in an emergency.

No load funds have neither a front end load or deferred sales charge. It is important to know who is managing these funds and what service you will receive.

You may purchase Mutual Funds from a Financial Consultant who works for an independent Broker and who sells funds from many companies, or from a 'captive' sales person who has the choice of only one company's products.

Presently there are over 600 Mutual Funds being sold in Canada and more funds are being developed all the time.

BENEFITS OF MUTUAL FUNDS

1. **Mutual Funds or Stocks benefit from dollar cost averaging.** Because the values go up and down, sometimes you are buying your shares at a lower cost and sometimes at a higher cost when you set up a monthly plan. The average cost is used to decide how much the increase/decrease (Capital Gain/Loss) is when you want to sell them. Over five, ten, fifteen, or twenty years the increase is usually considerable.

   See next page for an example on how different market conditions affect a basic $100 a month plan.

2. **Compounding.** Compounding Interest or Dividends (as you receive with Mutual Funds) help you by regularly increasing the totals. It is easy to set up a monthly plan (P.A.C.) as an automatic withdrawal on your chequing account. It is good practice to deduct the investment at the beginning of the month, without fail, and use the rest of your money for expenses.

MUTUAL FUND DOLLAR COST AVERAGING

These charts show the different results you may obtain by investing $100 a month for 10 years in various market conditions. The results change because, when the market goes down and the amount of the investment stays the same, you buy more shares with the $100. At the end of 10 years when the market has gone up and down, you have purchased many more shares than if the market has consistently gone up.

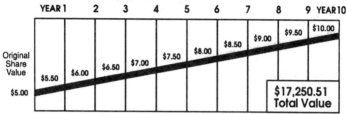

CONTINUOUSLY INCREASING PATTERN. Market consistently increases from $5 a share to $10 a share. The $12,000 investment increases to $17,250 – a 43.8% increase.

DOWN AND UP PATTERN. Market rises eventually to $10 with many fluctuations. The $12,000 is worth over $22,000 – a 83% increase.

PRICE RETURNS TO ORIGINAL VALUE AFTER CONSISTENT DOWN MARKET. The value of the shares never rise above $5. The $12,000 investment increases to over $25,455 – an increase of over 112%.

3. Professional management of a Mutual Fund means you do not need to make frequent decisions on when to buy or sell your investments.

4. Flexibility when adding or withdrawing money is available with Mutual Funds.

5. Mutual Funds hold shares in many companies, so your investment is diversified. Purchase two or more Mutual Funds for even greater diversification.

6. The Fund company sends you regular statements and tax receipts for your personal records.

7. Use Mutual Funds for your R.R.S.P. as long as they qualify under the R.R.S.P. rules. These qualifications include both Canadian content and the dollar limits defined by Revenue Canada.

YEARLY PLANS

You may deposit one yearly amount of $1,200 which would result in a little less money at age 65.

Example I
If at age 20, you deposited **$1,200** at the end of each year, at 12% return you would have **$1,629,876** after 45 years. Investing **$100** a **MONTH**, at 12% return after 45 years will give you **$2,145,649**. A difference of **$515,773!**

Example II
Starting at age 40, deposit $1,200 at the end of each year at 12% return. After 25 years you would have over **$160,000**. Invest **$100** a **MONTH** at 12% return. After 25 years you would have more than **$187,800**. A difference of approximately **$27,800!**

DIVERSIFICATION

When you have your emergency fund of three to six months income in a low risk, easily accessible place, you should start to look at diversification. Diversification may be achieved simply by starting another type of account. It does not have to be exotic, just different. Ask as many questions as you need to feel comfortable with your decisions.

LEARNING TO INVEST

You can start a Money Market, Bond, Equity or Mortgage Mutual Fund account with monthly contributions as low as $50 per month.

Starting one of these accounts is an excellent way to learn more about how investments work. Adding regular amounts may be subject to small fees, but is one of the best ways to consistently increase your Net Worth.

An account at a Brokerage Firm may be started for $1,000 or less (although higher fees may result due to purchasing less than 'board lots' of 100 shares in each company). It is also difficult to obtain diversification with Stocks when you have small amounts to invest.

REINVESTING DIVIDENDS
AND INTEREST

Compounding is necessary to maximize the increase on your investments. You need to reinvest your Interest, Dividends, and Capital Gains each year so there is a larger amount on which to receive returns. It is so easy to take out the increase each year. If you do, you lose one of the best ways to increase your Net Worth.

Chapter Ten

RETURNS ON YOUR INVESTMENTS

THREE WAYS TO GAIN

There are only three ways to receive returns on your invested money: Interest, Dividends, and Capital Gains. It is important to know in what form your returns are because they are taxed differently.

INTEREST

Interest is a fixed or variable percentage of the total investment. It can be paid monthly, quarterly, semi-annually, annually or after a number of years. This is money that you lend to someone: a relative, a bank, trust company, credit union or insurance company. In return, they pay you a set percentage. This is a debt investment because your investment is someone else's debt.

COMPOUNDING

When your return is for several periods of time, the interest is added to the principal each period and the interest calculated on this greater amount. This is called compounding.

Compounding makes a longer term investment have a higher interest return than if you only earned interest on the principal amount. Remember the example from Chapter 6. The interest on $100 for one year is 12% so you would receive $12 interest. If your $100 at 12% was compounded monthly you would receive $12.68 interest. This may not seem like much but take the larger amount of $10,000 and compound this over ten years. Yearly compounding gives you approximately $25,900, while monthly compounding gives you over $27,000. This is an increase of over $1,100 in ten years.

 When your investments are interest bearing, you want to compound that interest as often as possible. When you are paying interest, you want to have it compounded as seldom as possible.

DIVIDENDS

Dividends are the profits paid from the Stocks or Mutual Funds that you own.

Each year a company makes a profit they decide how much to keep for future growth and expenses, and how much to pay out to their shareholders. People buy shares in companies to obtain part of the profits or have the share values increase. Their goal is to buy shares in companies that make sufficient profits so they have yearly income from these profits, or their Dividends will be reinvested so they have more shares in the company.

One benefit of receiving Dividends is the way that Revenue Canada taxes them. You are eligible for a 'Dividend Tax Credit' which may possibly reduce the taxes you pay on these returns significantly, depending on your income tax bracket. Check with your Financial Consultant on how this works.

CAPITAL GAINS

When you buy something and sell it for a higher price, the difference is called a Capital Gain.

Buy anything; paintings, gems, stamps, cars, houses, other property, antiques, companies or shares of companies. Sell for a higher price and you have a Capital Gain.

If you bought a painting at a junk shop for **$50** and later you discovered that it was a Renoir and you sold it for **$100,050**, the **$100,000** you make would be a Capital Gain.

In Canada, you would be taxed on the **$100,000** but **at present**, you would be able to use your lifetime Capital Gains Exemption of **$100,000** and pay no tax on this amount.

If you sold the same painting for **$300,050**, you would have to pay taxes on your gains over **$100,000** using the current method of $100,000 lifetime Capital Gains Exemption and 75% of the remaining gain ($200,000) taxed at your current income tax rate. This is still better than being taxed on the total amount.

BORROWING TO INVEST

Have you ever borrowed to invest? You may think the answer is "no", but you may be surprised to find out the answer is "yes!" The purchase of your home may not be thought of as an investment, but it certainly can be. A mortgage on your home is money borrowed so you may invest it in your home.

You can use the same principle by borrowing to invest in other things such as Mutual Funds. A Mutual Fund is a better 'risk' than purchasing items you will be using and which will lose value such as clothes or even appliances. There is a tax break for the interest you pay on the loan. The value of the Mutual Fund should increase over a five to seven year time span. An investment loan is often at a lower rate of interest than credit card charges, or even standard loans at a Financial Institution because they are secured by more collateral (the Mutual Funds) than the amount of the loan.

Example

You borrow $10,000 and invest the total amount in two fairly conservative Canadian equity Mutual Funds. The interest on your loan of 10% per year ($1,000) is a tax deduction. If you are in the 43% tax bracket, the actual cost of this money is $570 or 5.7%.

If you are in the 50% tax bracket, your cost would only be $500 for the interest on your loan. By averaging 12% return on the $10,000 invested, you would be gaining 6% per year.

Tax regulations may change at anytime so see your Financial Consultant on how this idea could work for you.

Consider what will happen if your investment earns an average 12% return for ten years. You will be ahead 6 to 7%. Now, if the Government took the same amount as usual for income taxes, you would only be a little farther ahead. However, since Mutual Funds or Stocks gain mostly Dividend and Capital Gains, you are taxed at a lower rate on your returns from this investment.

THE GOVERNMENT'S SHARE

Check Chapter 21 on 'How Investments are Taxed' for information on how Interest, Dividends and Capital Gains are taxed. When investing any money, it is important to know how you are going to be taxed on it. An investment taxed at your normal rate gains you less than if you invested in ways that are taxed more beneficially.

"What is the risk involved in this investment?"

QUESTIONS TO ASK
YOUR FINANCIAL ADVISOR

1. What type(s) of returns will I receive from this investment?:
   a. Interest   **b.** Dividends   **c.** Capital Gains

2. How long should I hold this investment?

3. What is the risk involved in this investment?

4. How often will I receive information from my Financial Consultant or the company in which I invested? (At least every six months is necessary.)

GOAL SETTING

MY PERSONAL GOALS ARE: **I WILL NEED**

1. _____ $ _____
2. _____ $ _____
3. _____ $ _____
4. _____ $ _____
TOTAL $ _____

MY FAMILY GOALS ARE: **I WILL NEED**

1. _____ $ _____
2. _____ $ _____
3. _____ $ _____
4. _____ $ _____
TOTAL $ _____

MY FINANCIAL GOALS ARE: **I WILL NEED**

1. _____ $ _____
2. _____ $ _____
3. _____ $ _____
4. _____ $ _____
TOTAL $ _____

Chapter Eleven

INFLATION

Inflation is the yearly increase needed to purchase your needs. Deflation is a decrease in this same cost. In our experience, inflation has been the most common trend. However, look at the cost of televisions, refrigerators, freezers or computers in relation to their cost as a percentage of our annual income. Improved production methods, competition and greater use by the general population has brought these costs down. Lately, the resale value of many homes has decreased, making them more accessible to many people.

HOW INFLATION WORKS

Inflation works both for you and against you, often at the same time. A perfect example of inflation helping you, is the home you purchased in 1960 for $10,000 that is sold 33 years later for $100,000. This translates into an inflation rate of just over 7%. This looks like an extremely good 'investment' until you realize that, if you had invested the $10,000 in a solid Mutual Fund, you could you could have averaged over 10% per year, compounded, which would give you a present day total of about \$232,000.

You need a place to live anyway, and you probably did not pay for the home outright, and this makes your primary residence a practical 'investment'.

THE MARKET VS. THE SALE VALUE OF YOUR HOME

Don't confuse the 'market value' of your home with inflation. Market value depends upon many things such as area of the city, the city itself, and whether or not there is a 'buyers' or 'sellers' market in your city at a particular time. A popular market can suddenly change. The real value of your home or other property is the actual price you obtain for it when you want to sell.

Inflation works against you when you are living on a fixed or almost fixed income. Your spending dollars remain low and the expenses for food and other necessities go up and up. The result is less money to spend.

Inflation is the culprit when you pay \$1.00 for a loaf of bread which cost you 8¢ fifty years ago.

INFLATION WORKS FOR YOU WHEN:

1. The value of something you own is increased.

2. Your income is tied to the 'cost of living' rate (inflation).

3. What you own (your home), increases in value more than the cost to replace it.

4. You pay a bill with inflated dollars for an item you purchased with deflated dollars. You may contract to pay someone $12,000 five years from now for an item which you use. You will then pay in depreciated dollars which would be about 75% of each dollar in comparison to today's dollar.

INFLATION WORKS AGAINST YOU WHEN:

1. You are on a fixed income such as a pension which is not indexed, child support payments or alimony which does not include a 'cost of living' factor.

2. You decide to purchase a home or car and the price is too high for the real value to you.

3. The return on your investments does not keep up to the inflation rate.

**Understanding inflation will give you
an advantage for planning.**

Chapter
Twelve

BORROWING MONEY

A personal loan is different from a credit card because you go directly to a Financial Institution and apply. It could also be for a large ticket item such as a car and you make an application through the Automobile Finance Company.

The interest on a loan is often lower than a credit card. This is of real benefit since loans are set up over a definite period of time; the payments are consistent and all the principal is paid off when you have made all your payments on time.

When applying for a loan, take a list of your Assets and Liabilities (Net Worth Statement), also a copy of one of the latest income slips from your pay cheque.

Know the reason for the loan. If you are including some consolidation of your bills or credit cards, you should have the latest statements with you. If the loan is for a new purchase, know the exact price.

BE SURE YOU NEED TO BORROW

A decision to borrow may be made when interest rates are low or you are offered a special low interest rate. Read the small print because sometimes these 'loss leaders' have very stringent terms. All the money may be due if you miss a payment. The term may be for only one year then you must make a 'balloon payment' to cover the balance of your account. This usually means refinancing for you and may not be easy to do.

Wise use of a low interest rate loan may enable you to earn more on your investments than the interest rate on your purchase will cost you.

USING CREDIT TO YOUR ADVANTAGE

You must decide how you want to use credit and wisely incorporate your decisions into your everyday spending habits. Your spending can ruin your life; or you can make intelligent use of credit to make your life easier and more fulfilling.

If, at some point, you cannot pay the entire amount for the month, read the contract or bill. You may be able to reduce the credit charges by paying 50% and pay no interest on that portion of the bill. If you have several charge accounts, pay the ones with the highest interest rates first. You must be careful when using credit this way. It is very easy to allow the balance to increase month to month.

Credit is like a passport. You never think of getting it until it is needed; then you are stuck until it comes through.

KNOW YOUR CREDIT RATING

In order to be approved for credit, you need a credit rating in good standing. If you presently do not have any credit rating, take a small loan with a Financial Institution even if you do not need the money. Repay the loan promptly and you have established your own credit rating. Whatever your marital or family situation, you always need to have a personal credit rating established.

Credit can assist you in your lifestyle; or it can be a weapon that is lethal in its power, keeping you entangled long after you have worn out, broken, or discarded the items you purchased.

Chapter Thirteen

CREDIT

It is difficult to operate without credit in today's society. However, you need to use credit to your advantage. Some people do not have any credit and do not want any. Others use credit since they own a home with a mortgage or a car with a loan against it. Often people have so many credit cards, they do not know how much credit they really do have. Credit cards come in a variety of styles, types and obligations.

RULES FOR CREDIT CARDS

1. Read the contract which comes with the card and **KEEP** it in a safe place to reread whenever necessary.

2. Know the interest rate on each card and the annual fee. If there is an annual fee and a lower interest rate, you should know how much the average balance would have to be, to counteract the amount of the fee.

3. Decide how you are going to use credit:
   - Charge all purchases and pay total or partial balance monthly.
   - Charge all gas and pay total or partial payment each month.
   - Charge on various store cards and pay in full or partial balance each month.
   - Charge only for special occasions such as holidays or birthdays and pay the full or partial balance monthly.
   - Decide in advance how much you are going to spend on each person for each occasion. **Do not go over this budget.**

4. Make a list of all your credit cards and their account numbers and keep it in a place separate from your credit cards.
   - Check your credit card statements and verify them against your purchase slips.
   - A credit card service will call the companies where you have credit cards in case of loss or theft.

TYPES OF CREDIT CARDS

Charge Cards are debts you pay off each month and for which you qualify more easily than other types of credit. Often they have no limit, or a very high limit.

Revolving Credit Cards have a limit and you must make at least a partial payment each month when there is a balance.

Store Credit Cards have very high interest rates, often 28.8% per year, figured at 2.4% per month. (P.S: If you find an investment that pays **you** 28.8% a year guaranteed, please tell us).

Specialty Cards are cards which are used only for certain types of purchases; for example, dining at good to excellent restaurants or used for travel such as airplane fares and accommodations.

Cheque Cashing Cards are not credit but are used to allow you to cash cheques at stores.

Debit Cards directly debit to your bank account and as yet are not used a great deal in Canada.

The 'Friendly' Store card is the one where you purchase their merchandise on credit. However, often these stores have an agreement in place to 'sell' these contracts to a Finance Company which can charge up to 32% interest on the account and may be extremely obnoxious when you are late for a payment.

Consumer protection legislation prohibits harassment to collect overdue payments. For instance, calls at your place of employment or to your home late at night or early morning are considered harassment.

Sometimes, the store has an agreement with a credit company which does all the credit for that store and several other stores as well. Several stores may use the same Finance Company. The difficulty with this is, if you are refused credit from one store, you will be refused credit from all stores that use the same Finance Company.

Know the due dates of all your credit obligations and pay them by that date. Additional interest is charged at high rates for being even one day late.

LOANS FROM THE BANK, TRUST COMPANY, OR CREDIT UNION

The loans you obtain from a financial institution such as a Bank, Trust Company or Credit Union usually have the lowest rate of interest. There is a set repayment schedule and there can be a variety of terms and conditions. Most of the time you may repay these loans ahead of schedule.

SMALL LOANS

Institutions for the most part, do not write loans for small amounts of $1,000 or less. They suggest you apply for a credit card to handle this for you. This is all very well, but remember how high the interest rate is on credit cards. Perhaps it would be more beneficial to obtain a larger loan to meet with the banks' minimum and pay it off as soon as possible. Or, use the additional loan amount to pay off all your store cards and other credit cards. Just remember not to use them until you have this loan paid in full!

A LINE OF CREDIT

Financial Institutions have another type of credit that you may want to research. It is the Line of Credit. This is really a preset maximum with no interest charged until you write a cheque against the account. The Line of Credit is either 'unsecured' or 'secured' with your home or other investments as collateral. A lower interest rate is available when the Line of Credit is 'secured'. Be sure you want to put this security up for collateral, because if you default on the payments, the Financial Institution may legally repossess your collateral.

KNOWING YOUR CREDIT CARDS

The importance of knowing the particulars of your credit cards starts when you decide to use them. If possible, choose the card which carries the lowest percentage interest on it. You may decide to 'pay down' a larger amount than usual on an account to reduce the credit charge. If you are only able to pay some of your cards, decide to make a payment on those cards that carry the highest interest.

Know the 'due dates' of all your credit cards and bills and send out postdated cheques for the due date. There is no penalty as long as the cheque arrives well before the due date. Most big companies have a date file that they use for these payments. You save on the credit charges because the bill is paid on time and you obtain all the interest from the chequing account until the cheque is cleared. Some Financial Institutions have new services which allow you to call them the day the bill is due and have the money taken from your chequing account.

SHOULD YOU GO FOR GOLD?

Gold cards are very popular and sometimes have benefits attached. Make sure you need these benefits before you order a Gold card. There is usually a higher yearly fee and sometimes higher interest rates. It is never a good idea to get a Gold card if there is no real benefit for you. An annual charge, with a lower rate has no benefit to you if you pay off your cards every month. Calculate the 'break even' point – the point where the reduced interest actually does lower your costs, decide on what amount you could charge and leave on the account without negative results for you.

REPAYING CREDIT CARDS

Make your payments higher than the minimum payment if possible. For instance, if your balance is $1,000 on a store credit card and the interest rate is 2.4% per month, the interest you pay comes to $24 for the month. A payment of $30 reduces the debt by $6. Make a payment of $50 and you have paid $26 off the principal. It would take you over nine years to pay off the $1,000 debt by paying $30 a month, and only a little over two years by paying $50 a month.

 A 'rule of thumb' is to add at least the current month's interest charge to your minimum payment.

KNOW YOUR CREDIT RATING

Every area in Canada has a credit bureau service to whom you can write and obtain a copy of your credit history. You must send them proof of who you are, your Social Insurance Number, address, legal name and must personally sign the letter. Obtain the local address by calling either the Credit Bureau listed in the telephone directory or by calling Equifax for the local address. Question any incorrect fact and, if the creditor agrees, your report will change. If you had a difference of opinion with a creditor – you withheld payments due to lack of service or poor quality merchandise – you can submit your version which will be added to your file.

Chapter
Fourteen

THE BIGGEST LOAN OF ALL: YOUR MORTGAGE

Most Canadians still want to live in property they personally own. Whether or not this is a good/wise investment depends on many factors; some which are logical and some which are emotional.

Real estate, including residential real estate, increased in value at an average rate of around 6% over the last two decades. After 1988, Real Estate values decreased in most areas of Canada. This caused many people to suffer what may be called a 'paper loss' of their asset base. However, only when you actually sell your home does the 'loss' become real.

YOUR CHOICES
There are two decisions to make when deciding to purchase a home or condominium where you will personally live.

1. Is the cost of owning a home a realistic way to manage my basic shelter costs?

2. Am I a person who feels more comfortable as a home owner, or is living in rented space an option I would enjoy?

When **purchasing** a home you must make some additional decisions. Location and type of home (condo, semi-detached, single family, large or small property/home) are very important. You will have more difficulty changing your mind and selling than you would have in changing rental accommodations.

CONDOMINIUM COSTS

When you decide to purchase a condominium, you must include the condominium fees in your estimates. These can range from modest to very high. Be sure you have a clear understanding of these fees and have a written contract for what the fees cover.

COMPARING COSTS

To compare home ownership with rental accommodation, you must choose the same neighbourhood, and the same type of unit. It is sometimes very difficult to do this.

HOME/CONDO OWNERSHIP
- Mortgage
- Condo Fees
- Taxes
- Heat/hydro
- Maintenance

RENTAL UNITS
- Rent
- Heat/hydro
- Parking

BASE YOUR DECISIONS
ON REALITY

There are other considerations as well as cost. If you have children, single or semi-detached homes seem to be more accommodating than a high rise rental unit, although many children have been successfully raised in apartment buildings.

Once you have estimated the fixed costs, there is the tricky estimation of two items; repairs and maintenance, and equity in your home (which can only be estimated until you actually sell).

If you are a single person or a single parent, you must make a decision whether you want the responsibility of maintenance and repairs.

THE IMPACT OF INFLATION

In the past, some people financed their retirement due to inflation, which resulted in the increased value of their homes. This may not happen in the future.

FINANCING YOUR HOME

Financing your home from your own savings is very commendable but usually not practical. When purchasing a home, most people will need a mortgage to pay a portion of the cost.

MORTGAGES

MORTGAGES are legal contracts and therefore you must be sure of your decisions **before** you sign **anything**. You have the right to shop for the best terms, to have all your questions answered and to deal with mortgage grantors who treat you with respect.

AMORTIZATION PERIOD

The 'amortization' period is the amount of time over which the debt is to be repaid. This is usually over 20, 25, or 30 years but can be shorter.

THE TERM OF THE MORTGAGE

The 'term' of the mortgage in Canada is how long the interest rate is in effect. This is usually for a six month, one year, two year, three year, four year, five year, seven year, or ten year period. In other countries the TERM and the AMORTIZATION PERIOD are for the same amount of time.

MORTGAGE TERMS

There are also **'open'** or **'closed'** mortgages.

'Open' means that you MAY pay off the balance at any time during the term without penalty.

'Closed' means extra payments may only be made under specific conditions which are laid out in the contract.

TWO TYPES OF CLOSED MORTGAGES

1. You make only the payments required in the agreement and the whole amount is due at the end of the term. If there is a balance, this amount may be remortgaged using the latest interest rates and allows you to negotiate new terms and conditions.

2. A pre-determined payment schedule with an optional additional payment. This amount is usually up to 10% or 15% of the original mortgage amount and paid either within each year of your contract or on a specific date such as the renewal date.

INTEREST RATES

A **FIXED** rate is set at the beginning of the contract for the duration of the mortgage contract.

A **VARIABLE** rate is one which goes up and down with the prime rate and is set at one or two percentage points above the prime rate.

A **BLENDED** rate is often used for remortgaging where you are taking an old mortgage and adding a new mortgage to it. If you were paying 10.5% on $50,000 and added $50,000 at 8% interest, the blended rate would be 9.25% on the new mortgage.

PAY DOWN YOUR MORTGAGE

Pay down your mortgage faster by making a payment every two weeks or twice a month. You reduce your amortization time from 25 years to around 19 years and pay very little more per year while doing this. The interest you save over six years is more than $50,000!

When interest rates decrease and you renegotiate your mortgage for a lower rate; keep your monthly payments the same as they were at the higher interest rate. You were making the old payments and if you continue the same payments, you save again. Depending on your old interest rate and how much your old payments were, you may be able to reduce your amortization time to 16, 14 or even 12 years, thus saving many thousands in interest.

THE DIFFERENCE OF PAYING ONE PERCENT LESS ON YOUR MORTGAGE

Corrine bought her home and was lucky to get her mortgage at 10% two years ago. Her payments on the $100,000 mortgage are about $918 per month. Over the 25 years she is repaying her loan, she will pay back just over $275,400 if she keeps the 10% mortgage rate.

Ann purchased her home this year and her $100,000 mortgage is carried at 9% for the same 25 years. Her payments are slightly over $848. She will pay back a little over $254,500 and save over $20,000 because her mortgage interest is 1% less.

 Take advantage of all these ideas to magnify your savings and have more money to invest! Shop for the lowest interest rate and the best repayment terms.

Chapter
Fifteen

PURCHASING A CAR

So you need a new car! Women as a rule are very careful shoppers when it comes to cars. Before you go to any car dealership, make some decisions. It is easy to buy a bigger, flashier car or pay a higher price than you can afford when you are under pressure in the showroom. Decide upon the total cost of the car and how much you can afford in payments before you walk in the door. What features do you need in the car; transmission, power steering and brakes, automatic steering, air conditioning or the very basic model? Are you going to be travelling alone or with children?

SHOP FOR THE DEALER AS WELL AS THE CAR

Go to see several dealers. Check the reputation of the dealership with friends or associates who have purchased a car in the past year. Be aware of how the salesperson asks questions and responds to your questions. You may think your relationship with the salesperson is a short term one. It is not when you get a good salesperson. He/She will help you get good service and make sure you are satisfied with the car.

RESEARCH

Take brochures home with you. Decide on colour and accessories at home. Once you have decided on your preferred model, call or go to several other dealerships with the same model. When you compare costs you may realize significant savings; this means money in your pocket.

How important is the colour to you? Do you really need power windows? Order what **you** want. If extra options like power locks, cruise control, tilt steering wheel, etc., are not important to you, look on the lot for cars that were demonstrators or executive driven cars. They MAY have a lower price or extra options at no significant cost to you. However, these cars cannot have the replacement cost auto insurance (see Chapter 16).

Your research should include the Consumer's Report and the 'Lemon-Aid' Book written by Phil Edmonston.

HOW TO NEGOTIATE
WITH THE DEALERSHIP

Some dealerships currently are going to the 'No Dicker Sticker', where the price is not negotiable. Many dealers still use the negotiating system. The salesperson goes between you and the 'manager' negotiating the price, which options are included and other details.

YOU have the final say in your purchase. **Be tough!** Have **your** price in mind and do not go over it. If you feel pressured say: *"Thanks for your time"* or *"I'll think about it"* and walk away. Go to another dealership. Try another part of the city. Go to a nearby small town. Keep looking.

BARGAIN INTEREST RATES

The 1.9% or 2.9% interest rate you see in newspaper advertisements may or may not be a bargain. If you take the low interest rate option, be prepared to pay the sticker price on the car. Also be sure you read the contract carefully and understand all the terms. If you finance elsewhere, you are able to negotiate your purchase price. Your interest rate may be higher and the purchase price lower. You must find the 'best deal' for you.

FIXED OR VARIABLE
INTEREST RATE

A variable rate of financing means that your payment will go up and down when the interest rate fluctuates. Usually on a loan, the variable rate is lower than the fixed rate. If the rates are low, you can benefit by taking the variable rate option and making additional payments on the loan. The extra money you save due to the lower rate can be deposited in a special account for use when interest rates rise.

Sometimes you can even renegotiate your loan when the rates increase. You want the payments to be reasonable, so they don't interfere too much with your lifestyle. On the other hand, you want to pay the car off as fast as possible.

NEW OR USED VEHICLE?

When you drive a new car off the lot, your car immediately depreciates. A used car becomes a viable option but it is an option that may have some potholes for you. There are some good buys in the used car market, but also some real lemons! You must be careful and trust your instincts and your mechanic. Yes, take any car in which you are really interested to your mechanic. You should also make sure you buy a car which has had its safety check. These precautions will not prevent getting a lemon (some new cars are also lemons), but they lower your chances.

BUY OR LEASE?

Most people have continued to purchase their cars even if they must use credit to attain their goal. Leasing can be a good option, but there are some pitfalls. Make sure you know how much driving you do each year since a lease has a built in clause that usually charges per kilometre after a base amount. Drivers who put high mileage on their cars pay extra at the end of a lease or are put into the position of having to buy the vehicle at that time.

One benefit you may enjoy is the interest rate may be lower on the lease than on an outright purchase. If you are in business for yourself, you can write off the entire lease payment to a set maximum per year. When you purchase outright, only the interest portion is eligible for write off.

SAFETY FEATURES

Anti lock brakes and driver/passenger air bags are good safety features and should be included in your deal if possible. A woman who drives alone much of the time should consider automatic door locks and power windows. This is a safety feature and **not** a luxury.

WARRANTY

What type of warranty is included when you purchase your car? Or does the car dealer want you to add to your costs by purchasing an 'extended term' warranty? An extended warranty is not usually necessary for a reliable new car and is very expensive insurance.

MILEAGE COSTS

Find out the miles per gallon or the litres per kilometre. Fuel consumption is a significant part of your monthly expenses if you do a lot of travelling.

Chapter Sixteen

AUTO INSURANCE

The goal of insurance is to never have to use it.

The premium for auto insurance is based on several things.

1. Driving record. How long you have been driving and your age (under 25 the premium is higher).

2. Driver education. The premium is lowered for the first three years, provided you don't have an "at fault" accident during that period.

3. Use of the vehicle and the purpose – business, short or long distances to school or work. Once again, you must tell the insurance company when your usage changes.

4. Tickets, accidents or other claims.

SHOP FOR YOUR AGENT

Look for professionals who answer questions and assist you through any claims. Assistance with claims is very important.

You have the option of using a 'direct' carrier or a 'broker' the same as Home/Tenants insurance. Often the same company carries both types of insurance. Choose the insurance company carefully with your Broker or Agent.

You NEVER want to make a claim, but if you must, you want the process to be expeditious and hassle free. Sometimes a company that was good in the past about handling claims is poor now, and the company that was poor in the past may have excellent service. If you do not get the service you require, change companies or brokers. You may get a discount for several years with the same company, but this is not worth much if you have problems when you need to collect.

Brokers may call various insurance companies and get quotes for you. The quotes will be the same for any Broker. Go to the Broker or Agent that gives you the best service. Ask questions even if you know the answers, to give you an understanding of how you may be treated.

Auto insurance plans are controlled by each province. There are regional differences but the process of making informed decisions and knowing as much as you can is the same.

**ASK QUESTIONS, WRITE DOWN THE
ANSWERS, NOTE THE DATE AND
TO WHOM YOU ARE TALKING.**

Should you carry collision when the value of the car is so low that the deductible eliminates any claim? There are three situations where you lose when you have no collision insurance:

1. If you are hit by an unknown driver and there is no collision on your car, you cannot submit a claim.

2. If you are hit by someone with no insurance, there is no coverage for you unless you have collision coverage.

3. If the accident is your fault.

WAIVER OF DEPRECIATION does not mean your car does not depreciate but does mean that **IF YOU BUY A NEW CAR** and you 'total'it, you get the price you paid for it less the deductible, within the time limit specified – usually 24 or 30 months. Your car **MUST BE BRAND NEW** to qualify – not a 'demonstrator'.

LOSS OF USE

If you depend on your car for work or on a regular basis, you need Loss of Use coverage. It can take two to three weeks to get a badly damaged car repaired, so you need to rent a car for this time. This can cost you $20 - $30 per day. If you have Loss of Use, this is covered. As soon as you are notified your car is ready or you find a suitable replacement, you no longer qualify for Loss of Use coverage and you must pay the rent yourself, even if you do not have the use of your own vehicle because of a safety check or dealer preparation.

ABSTAINERS POLICY means you **must** abstain completely from all alcoholic beverages.

If the Abstainers policy was in effect at the time of an accident, and you were found to be impaired, your insurance would not cover you or your vehicle, but would cover who you hit. This is the same for all other policies.

LIABILITY INSURANCE

LIABILITY INSURANCE is usually purchased for $1,000,000. This means if you are responsible for the accident you are covered for up to $1,000,000 of liability. *CLAIMS* may be filed up to one year after the accident.

DISCOUNTS
• Multi vehicle.
• Mature insured.
• Non drinkers of alcohol, except at communion.
• Good driver rating – six ****** star or better.

You may not get the best premium if you allow other people to drive your car. An accident involving YOUR car affects YOUR rates.

You cannot insure every situation. For some things, you may have to self-insure.

COVERAGE IS ELIMINATED

There is no insurance coverage if you forget to renew your driver's licence or if your licence is suspended because of unpaid fines, whether you realize it or not. In Ontario they can suspend your licence if fines are not paid. When your licence is suspended, **you have no insurance.**

If you are charged with impaired driving there is no insurance on your own vehicle, but they will pay for the repairs on the other vehicle(s) in the accident, or in Ontario, the Direct Compensation Property Damage will pick up the damaged car insurance.

The insurance company expects you to be a responsible citizen, and if you don't pay your fines, you are not being responsible! The insurance company can either deny you coverage, or charge an extra premium for your insurance. In Ontario, the government provides a "Facility" pool for drivers or risks that insurance companies won't take. The premium is significantly higher. Other companies will not look kindly on your claims record, so it is recommended that you not change your insurer for three to five years after a claim, especially if you qualify for a *'forgivable'*. A forgivable is when you have an accident, but since you have been a GOOD long term driver, they *forgive* your accident and you keep your 5 or 6 star rating with that company. If you go elsewhere, you usually start over with a '0' star rating.

HOW ACCIDENTS AFFECT YOUR INSURANCE COSTS

Usually, if you have one accident and if you were a 6 ****** star driver, you become a 5 ***** star driver for five years. A second accident will put you back to 0 star again, and you will have to work up to 6 ****** star again over the next six years.

If you had a couple of comprehensive claims, the insurance company would increase your deductible. If you had several claims such as five windshield breakage claims, the insurance company could eliminate the glass coverage portion of your insurance.

TICKETS CAN INCREASE
YOUR INSURANCE COSTS

TICKETS are not registered against you until paid or you are convicted by the courts. If you decide to fight the charge, it may not even get on your record and therefore is not counted against your policy. This may be something to remember if you have a streak of tickets and your insurance renewal date is approaching.

RECOMMENDATIONS

1. Do not claim for small accidents - under $400.

2. Be sure to keep your driver's licence and all your tickets paid and up to date.

3. Do not allow others to drive your car. They may incur an accident which will affect the cost of your insurance. Tickets go on a driver's licence except for the new photo radar which will record the car's licence plate and so charge the owner of the car.

DEDUCTIBLES

Usual deductions are $250 for collision and $100 for comprehensive insurance. The usual public liability coverage is for $1,000,000.

THE UMBRELLA POLICY

Professional women may want $2,000,000 or an even greater amount of public liability insurance. This can be purchased under an 'umbrella' policy which will cover all personal hazards, e.g. house, cottage, boat, cars. This insurance is less expensive because it uses one coverage for liability on all your property.

Chapter Seventeen

HOME INSURANCE

When deciding on your **'RISK'** coverage, first look for a professional who explains the options, asks questions about what you need, and gives you good answers. The goal of any insurance is to cover you financially in times of crisis. You are usually under extreme stress when living through a crisis so it is not the time to realize you didn't ask enough questions or understand some important answers in regard to your coverage.

You can deal with a **'direct writer'** who works for one company and sells only that company's policies, or you can go to a **'broker'** who deals with many companies and who chooses the policy they think is most suitable for your needs at the best price.

In home/tenants insurance you need to know exactly what you must have covered by the policy.

Example
Know the value of your home and the approximate value of the contents. Do you own special items that may need to be identified in the policy or need additional coverage? (For example; camera equipment, jewellery, fine art or other valuables.)

There are two types of coverage: **'Broad Form'** which covers the *named perils* on contents and *all risk* on the building or: **'Comprehensive'** which covers *all risk* on building AND contents subject to policy exclusions and your deductible. Watch for limits on jewellery if you have expensive items. Your Broker can tell you if it should be insured on a jewellery schedule.

Be sure that water damage and sewer backup are covered on your policy where applicable if you have any sewer drains or sump pumps in your home. To some insurance companies, 'water damage' also means water backing up or escaping from eavestroughs or downspouts, and the melting of snow or ice on the exterior of the roof. Find out what your company is covering.

GUARANTEED REPLACEMENT
Guaranteed Replacement means you can replace the items at whatever it costs TODAY with similar style and materials. It is vital to identify what the building would cost to replace NOW and insure for the full amount of the replacement cost. The land is not included in this price. The cost to replace the building may be higher than the estimate, especially when it must be done quickly and builders know it is covered by insurance.

A Real Estate appraisal of the home may be very different than a replacement cost appraisal.

Antique furniture is extremely difficult to replace. A family heirloom table has no exceptional value to the insurance company and they will just replace it with a similar table.

INFLATION

Your policy must include an inflation rate that is also insured. The result is when inflation adds to the cost of replacement of your home, this increased cost is covered.

HOW TO KEEP ALL YOUR POSSESSIONS INSURED

You must let the insurance company know when you change or add to your home. If you build a sun room for $10,000 or finish your basement for $6,000, adding the replacement cost to your home will cost very little. However, if you don't add this cost, the replacement of these improvements will not be covered under your policy. Even repairing or rebuilding a new addition may be more than what it cost to build it. You may have done some work yourself or purchased bargain materials that may not be available if you must replace the structure due to fire or windstorm. Earthquake insurance may be purchased but it is very expensive.

The insurance company expects you to be a responsible citizen.

Coverage can be denied, or the deductible can be raised by the insurance company when you go to renew. Your record is studied prior to renewal each year, and your evaluation is based on a three year time frame.

If you have had several claims in the past three years, it can cost you more money or your coverage may be denied because you became a higher risk.

 You should think twice about putting in a claim for a bike that cost $300 when you have a $200 deductible. Small claims add to your record. If you need the coverage later because of a larger claim, the small claim adds unnecessarily to your three year record. This may increase your insurance costs significantly.

COVERING ALL YOUR ASSETS WITH INSURANCE

Rental units you own can be covered on your Home Owners Insurance Policy if they are single family or duplex units and not an apartment building. The liability portion of the insurance on your home can cover both which will reduce the total cost of insurance. Be sure to insure 'rental income,' as mortgage and taxes need to be paid even if the building is damaged and unfit for habitation. Check with your Agent or Broker for details.

TENANTS INSURANCE

When you rent, the building owner has insurance for the property which covers liability, fire, and theft of their goods. If you are shown to be responsible for a fire, say a grease fire, which spreads and causes damage and smoke damage to the entire building, your insurance company must pay. If you have no coverage, YOU must pay. Your personal possessions are never covered under a landlord's policy so you must have your own coverage.

CONDOMINIUM INSURANCE

Condominium coverage is similar to a Tenant's Package. You insure your contents and a separate policy is taken out by the condominium corporation to insure the building. Look for a policy with improvements and betterments, and include a 30% to 40% additional living expense instead of the usual 20% you normally buy on a tenants' package.

Most companies have policies especially for condominium owners, with Loss Assessment and Owners' Contingency coverage included. Your Broker will advise you on what you need.

SINGLE LIMIT COVERAGE

There is a new type of policy – Single Limit Coverage which is completely flexible. The coverage is calculated at twice the replacement cost of your home. Check it out with your Insurance Broker.

Comparison Claim Example

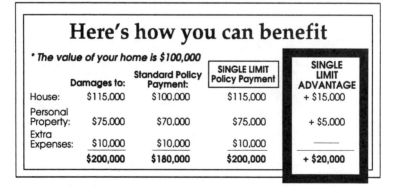

Here's how you can benefit

The value of your home is $100,000

	Damages to:	Standard Policy Payment:	SINGLE LIMIT Policy Payment	SINGLE LIMIT ADVANTAGE
House:	$115,000	$100,000	$115,000	+ $15,000
Personal Property:	$75,000	$70,000	$75,000	+ $5,000
Extra Expenses:	$10,000	$10,000	$10,000	———
	$200,000	**$180,000**	**$200,000**	**+ $20,000**

APPRAISE YOUR JEWELLERY

Jewellery appraisal is very important because under most policies, there is a set limit of around $2,000. Even a diamond ring would not be replaced with this limit, but only a professional appraisal tells you how much it really is worth. This is particularly true for antique jewellery and designer pieces. Jewellery also must be legal. For example, if you bring in a special ring from your American or European tour and you didn't pay the duty on it, there is no insurance on it.

WHAT DID YOU OWN?

There are inventory booklets available from some insurance companies which will help you identify all your possessions. The insurance claims adjuster will ask you what you had in your closet and in your dressers if they are destroyed by disasters such as fire or tornado. If there is nothing to remind you of what you owned, you may have difficulty proving your losses.

It is *your responsibility* to prove your case to the insurance company.

ACTION PLAN: Video cameras are easily available. It is a good idea to video tape each room, giving a commentary on the contents of each room as you film it. Photographs have always been accepted as evidence. Write down serial numbers.

Store this information in a different location than your house; at the office, a friend's place or in your safety deposit box. You could also purchase a fire proof box for storing all your records and valuables.

AN EASY MISTAKE YOU MAY MAKE

People who might share accommodation are not covered under one policy automatically – each person needs his/her own or all parties need to be named on one policy. For example, if a person starts a grease fire which causes $10,000 damage to your home and you have received payment for his/her room (shared cost), you must collect from him/her or pay for the damage yourself. This does not apply if someone is just visiting.

HOME/TENANTS INSURANCE DISCOUNTS

You may be able to obtain a reduction on your Home/ Tenants insurance premiums for one or more of the following conditions:

- New Homes
- Mature insureds
- Smoke detectors
- Neighbourhood Watch
- Alarms

- Security systems
- Fire extinguishers
- Non smokers
- No claims

*Ask your Broker what you can do to save money on your policy.

REMEMBER:

1. Be sure you have enough coverage under replacement costs to cover all increased values. Review policies every year and include any improvements, additions or new possessions.

2. You are obligated to tell the company about ANY changes. Otherwise, you are not insured for these items.

3. A small business in your home needs additional coverage. A fire which destroyed the stock of your craft business would not be covered under regular home/tenants insurance unless specified. Business policies should include your computer, software, records, etc. The insurance company could refuse to pay for a customer injured on your premises if you have no business liability insurance.

4. Baby sitting services in your home requires additional liability insurance and not many companies cover this risk. You must be operating within the law and have the proper licences and safety equipment and procedures to be able to apply for insurance.

5. You must turn in the bills and replace lost or stolen items to obtain the money. Sometimes the company will give you a preliminary cash advance but you must turn in the receipts to justify the payment.

6. The insurance company does not pay for home maintenance. If your leaking roof destroys some interior walls and possessions, you must replace the roof yourself and fix or replace the interior. You will not be compensated for any damage if the problem was caused by poor maintenance.

Chapter Eighteen

INSURANCE AND YOU

Canadians buy more life insurance than citizens of any other country in the world. Women own only a small percentage of all insurance sold.

Insurance, in simple terms, is used to create an estate for your living dependants.

Insurance companies sell many types of products. These include Life Insurance, Disability or Accident and Sickness Insurance, Annuities, Registered Retirement Plans, Registered Retirement Income Plans and Segregated Mutual Funds. Understanding what you have, what you need, and how you obtain what is best for you, is not usually a simple matter.

Determining the cost of life insurance is fairly simple if you know some basic rules. Your age, gender, smoking habits and health status, determine the cost of insurance for you. Deciding on what is included in your insurance package is where the fun begins!

The next step is to determine the length of time you want the policy to be in effect and whether you want the same premium for 5 years, 10 years, 25 years, to age 65, 71, or 100. Would you prefer to pay the policy in fewer years and keep the insurance in force without further premiums? The answers to these questions determine the type and term of the insurance policy and how much you pay monthly or yearly.

TYPES OF POLICIES:

TERM INSURANCE - The policy has the same premium for a specified period of time such as 5 years, 10 years, 20 years or Term to 100. There is no savings component in Term Insurance Policies and it tends to be the least expensive.

WHOLE LIFE - This type of policy includes a Savings, Dividend and Paid Up Addition Component. The policy may be paid up in a specific number of years such as 10 or 20, or continue for your lifetime. The return on the savings portion is usually not as good as if you invest the money yourself.

UNIVERSAL LIFE - A policy which combines a savings component with term insurance. The usual forms are yearly renewable term or term to 100. There may be a level 'death benefit' or an increasing 'death benefit'. A level 'death benefit' is for the face amount of the policy and increasing 'death benefit' includes the face amount plus the savings portion. It is cheaper than Whole Life Insurance and more expensive than straight Term Insurance, but it is more permanent than Term Insurance.

MORTGAGE INSURANCE - The face amount is decreased every year to match the decreased principal of your mortgage. This is usually not the best buy in the long run unless poor health precludes you from qualifying for less expensive insurance to cover your mortgage.

DIRECT MAIL INSURANCE - Guaranteed life insurance advertised in the media gives you a premium per month and an amount of insurance based on your age when you buy. The guarantee that your premium will never 'go up' is true, however your amount of coverage will decrease as you become older.

JOINT AND FIRST TO DIE
Pays at the first death and is often used for mortgage insurance to pay off the family home. Companies offer variations such as paying twice if both die within 31 days of each other. The survivor can take his/her own insurance out separately after the death of the first partner.

JOINT AND LAST TO DIE
This type of insurance is used in estate planning where one spouse has left everything to the other and there have been no tax problems. When the second spouse dies, the children inherit and may have to pay Capital Gains tax on the family cottage, business or other properties.

GROUP INSURANCE
If either partner is employed, you may have group insurance. You should know what is covered by reading the group insurance booklet which the company gives every employee.

This booklet explains the amount of life insurance there is on the husband, wife, children; how the extended health care works and how the drug portion operates. It will also explain if you have 'Out of Province' and 'Out of Country' insurance. There could be short term and long term disability insurance which covers employees when they become ill or are involved in an accident. Usually, a group insurance policy pays immediately for an accident and waits at least a week for coverage to begin for sickness.

NOTE: Always designate the beneficiary by name so loans and debts against the estate do not reduce the benefit to those for whom you want to provide.

Be sure you are specifically named in your spouse's insurance policy so the proceeds from the insurance come directly to you. Failure to do this would mean these proceeds would be tied up until the estate is probated. This might mean that you have no money for living expenses for several months.

Having a named beneficiary 'credit proofs' insurance money from bills and liabilities left by the deceased.

Chapter Nineteen

HEALTH INSURANCE

INDIVIDUAL INSURANCE

Disability insurance replaces income lost due to extreme illness or disability. Only people with earned income can apply. The costs vary greatly due to the type of job or position, length of coverage, how soon after your disability the coverage starts, and how young you are when the coverage begins.

The cost of disability insurance varies due to two factors.
1. How soon the payments start after your disability. Coverage can start as soon as 30 days or as long as 120 days.
2. The length of the coverage. If you decide on a two year plan, the cost is cheaper than if you want coverage for twenty years or until you are age 65.

The premium is also based on smoker status and occupation. Some occupations are not covered or are extremely expensive. People in what are considered 'dangerous jobs' have an expensive proposition when obtaining disability insurance.

GROUP INSURANCE

Disability insurance is often part of the Group Insurance package from your job and should be paid by your employer. Short term coverage usually starts on the first day for an accident, and on the eighth day for sickness, and continues for up to 17 or 26 weeks. Long term disability begins then and continues until the person recuperates or to the age specified in the policy.

OUT OF PROVINCE INSURANCE

Out of Province or Out of Country Coverage is included in some group insurance plans, or may be purchased separately by an individual. The coverage may look the same in all policies, but many policies have definite limitations.

Read all about pre-existing conditions and clauses. You may have coverage eliminated or reduced for mild conditions for which you visited a doctor previously. A pre-existing condition may not be covered under a policy. Check on this before you leave on vacation.

There are more than 25 different kinds of travel insurance for sale. Read the fine print. Call the issuer if you have any questions. You will want to know what is covered should you need to see the doctor or visit a medical facility while you are in another country.

Chapter Twenty

INCOME TAX

A large part of the financial support for our Government's activities and programmes comes from our Income tax. We have, however, the legal right to set up our finances so that we pay the least amount of tax possible, as long as we do not try to evade the tax we are required to pay.

This presents a challenge to you and gives you some opportunities.

In Canada there is a 'Progressive Income Tax' structure. Income tax increases from approximately 27% for the lowest amount of **taxable income** to 43% and continues up until you pay over 50% of your income in Tax. The Provincial Income Tax is different for every province and therefore, these numbers are approximate, but very close. For ease of reference, we will use 27%, 43% and 50% throughout the examples in the book. They may change with each new Budget, but most likely will not decrease.

101

REMEMBER: For every dollar you pay in income tax, you have not only lost that dollar, but lost whatever it could have grown to be.

REDUCING YOUR INCOME TAX BILL

The question becomes, "How do I reduce my Income Tax?"

1. Be sure to claim all your legitimate deductions. The people at Revenue Canada will **NOT** change your forms and add deductions you have missed.

   • You may go back and claim deductions you missed in previous years, if you send in an amendment. See your Financial Consultant or Accountant.

   • Take the equivalent to married exemption if you have dependent children and no spouse.

   • Plan your Medical, Dental, and Health care expenses, if possible. Remember, these expensesd o not have to be in a calendar year, but the expense year must end in the calendar year in which you are reporting.

Example

Keep all your medical expenses in one fiscal year which goes from any point in a year to 365 days later. For example: you had a lot of dental work (not paid by your Medical Plan) done in October to December one year. The next year in June, you bought new glasses; you have regular drug prescriptions filled every two months; and a child's orthodontist's care continues through the entire period. If anyone needs new glasses or prescriptions filled, get them any time before the end of the fiscal year (under your physician's guidance). Check to see if there are any other Health deductions that you could include in the same time frame.

Last Year Fiscal Year Begins	Current Year	End of Fiscal Year	Next Fiscal Year
October 1st	June August	September 30	October 1st

Buy your prescriptions and new glasses during this fiscal year

Every year you must subtract 3% of your Net Income before you may claim any deduction for medical expenses. If you spread these expenses over two years you will have two deductions instead of one. This reduces the amount you will save on your Income Tax.

 Include the cost of your medical plan as part of your deduction and also deduct any portion of your medical expenses, for example your deductible, not covered by your medical plan.

2. Set up your Investments so at least a percentage of them pay Dividends and increase in value (Capital Gains). These are taxed at a lower rate for most people. Even if the $100,000 lifetime tax free Capital Gains benefit is eliminated, presently Capital Gains are only taxed on 75% of the gain.

3. Keep all receipts related to business expenses and investments (include safety deposit box rental and interest paid to borrow money for investment purposes).

4. Think of starting a small business which will eventually produce a profit. Write off all expenses related to this business as well as expenses related to the amount of space and utilities you use in your home exclusively for your business.

5. Borrow money only to invest. This allows you to deduct the interest from your Income Tax Return. Borrowing money for investment purposes is a more complicated strategy but it makes more sense to borrow for items which could appreciate rather than for expendable items (clothes or restaurant meals) or depreciable items (cars, furniture, or appliances).

6. Contribute to your R.R.S.P. Where else can you attain a quick return of at least 27% as quickly as in two days? It is possible to deposit an amount into your R.R.S.P. one day within the eligible period and take it out anytime in January or February of the next year, and you will receive the full tax deduction. Of course, the purpose of setting up an R.R.S.P. is to provide for your retirement, but there are times when putting your money into a plan – then taking it right back out, is very smart.

Example

You have worked all year and you are laid off in November. Although you try to obtain a new job, you have no luck and feel you might have a significantly lower income for the next year. You might decide to go back to school or start your own small business and your earnings will not be as high for the next year.

Place your maximum R.R.S.P. contribution in an 'interest only' account. If needed, withdraw all or part of your plan. When you find a new job, move the remaining money into an investment with a higher Rate of Return.

You qualify for the income tax deduction, which is 27% or more and your money remains flexible. There may be a small fee to withdraw the money or close the account. Check this **before** you set up your account.

PROFESSIONAL TAX PREPARATION

It may benefit you to have your income tax prepared by a Professional. You must discuss what you are trying to do so the proper accounts can be set up. Submit the information early, since the last two or three weeks of April is not the time to expect any free time from a Tax Preparer. You may deduct the cost of having your taxes done professionally from your next year's tax bill.

Ask questions such as "What if I did XYZ, would that decrease my Income Tax?"

PAYING EXTRA TAXES

Some people like to receive a big tax rebate and pay extra taxes every year so they have a tax rebate. They use this 'found money' to pay off bills. Tell you what – give me that money and I will give you the same deal that Revenue Canada does. I will pay you no interest and give you your own money back 14 to 18 months later and I won't charge you anything to do this.

Would this money be better placed in your own investment plan? Even $25 a month makes a difference in your security when you retire. You could use it to pay off those 'end of the year debts' and save the credit charges of 16% – 28.8%. Still a good return on your money. Why put it where you cannot retrieve it when you need it and you receive absolutely no interest on it?

 Earn the most money possible, pay the least amount of taxes and at the latest possible time.

Chapter
Twenty One

WAYS TO SAVE
INCOME TAX

HOW INVESTMENTS ARE TAXED

Each type of return on your investments is taxed differently by Revenue Canada and this affects the net return of each type of investment.

INTEREST

Interest is simply added to your income and taxed at your highest rate. Example, if you are taxed at 27% on your income but the interest you received puts you up into the 43% tax bracket, you would be taxed at 43% on your interest income. On $100 of Interest income you would pay the government $43 instead of $27.

DIVIDENDS

Dividends on your Stocks or Equity Mutual Funds are subject to the 'Dividend Tax Credit'. This complex formula results in many people paying less taxes for Dividend income than their regular tax rate. To see the difference, calculate your tax in two ways. Firstly, as though all your investment returns were Interest, secondly, as though all your returns were Dividends.

CAPITAL GAINS

Capital Gains which qualify for the lifetime Capital Gains exemption are an even better tax bargain. Presently the first $100,000 of qualified Capital Gains are tax free. Real Estate no longer qualifies for this exemption. The remainder of your Capital Gains is split, with only 75% of the Capital Gains taxed at your regular tax rate. This means 25% of all Capital Gains are still tax free.

Use the tax laws and your investment knowledge to pay less tax on the returns from all your investments.

$1,000 return on investment	Different Tax Brackets		
	27%	43%	50%
INTEREST	$270	$430	$500
DIVIDENDS	Dividends are grossed up, then subject to the Dividend Tax Credit which reduces income tax on a sliding scale.		
CAPITAL GAINS 1	$0	$0	$0
CAPITAL GAINS 2	$202.50	$322.50	$375

Capital Gains 1 is the lifetime exemption of the first $100,000 of eligible Capital Gains.
Capital Gains 2 gains ineligible or in addition to those which qualify for the lifetime exemption.

The numbers on this chart are approximate. See your professional Financial Consultant or Tax Preparer for specifics on your tax obligations.

The result of changing your investments to those which receive Dividends or Capital Gains may be the reason you need to use a professional Tax Preparer or learn more about Income Tax yourself. The cost in money, time and effort is well worth it, if you gain higher net returns on your investments.

LEVERAGE

Borrowing money or paying interest on credit cards is a poor way to manage your money. There is one way to gain both increased returns on your money and have the government pay part of the cost. The way is to borrow money and put it in an investment which qualifies. This is called leveraging.

Investments which qualify include Stocks, many Mutual Funds, and companies. The challenge is to pick an investment which reduces risk and increases the opportunity of making good returns. Remember that interest bearing investments do not qualify.

Mutual Funds are a good investment for leverage because they provide:
1. Diversification
2. Professional Management
3. Flexibility

A leverage program is not complex but the commitment should be made for at least a five to seven year period. Investment values change with cycles of business and the economy. Sell your investment during an up market and not a down time or a low Stock Market. Since cycles are unpredictable, you need a flexible investment programme such as a well diversified portfolio of Mutual Funds. Although values may be down over one to two years, you will likely to do very well over five to seven years. You also need to be able to carry the costs of the investment through down markets with income from your job or other investments.

WHY LEVERAGE INCREASES YOUR RETURN AND REDUCES TAX

When you borrow to invest, there is a tax break on your interest costs.

Example

A woman borrows $10,000 to invest in Mutual Funds or Stocks. At 10% interest she pays $83 per month on her loan. Since the interest she pays is a tax deduction, and if she is in the 27% tax bracket, she will get a tax refund for $22, and so have a net cost of $61 per month.

After 10 years she decides to stop her leverage program. Her investments earned an average of 15% per year so her $10,000 has grown to about $40,000. She then repays the loan, and has $30,000 left. Her total cost was $7,320 in interest paid over the years, yet she now has more than four times that.

If she had invested $61 per month over 10 years – the same as her net interest payment – into the same funds, she would have only $17,091. This is almost $13,000 less than her leverage programme!

She has more money because the $10,000 has been growing for the whole 10 years. In the $61 per month investment plan, the first $61 has been growing for 10 years, but the rest has been there for less time – the last $61 for only one month.

Leveraging is not for everyone, however it makes more sense than buying clothes or even cars with credit. How many purchases are going to be around in 10 years?

POINTS TO REMEMBER
ABOUT LEVERAGING

1. Research the plan recommended to you.

2. Make a long term commitment.

3. Be sure to deduct the interest you pay on your loan from your taxes. You should apply for a reduction of income tax deducted where you work, so you do not need to wait until you file your annual return to receive your refund.

4. Read all the papers you sign from the bank. Understand the bank's rules.

5. If you pledge additional collateral for your loan, determine at what point in the growth of your funds it will not be needed. Remove it at that point. You will not be able to use your investment's collateral until it is no longer used as collateral.

6. Remember the additional net return when you invest your leverage program in Mutual Funds or Stocks. The returns on these investments are a combination of one or more of Dividends and Capital Gains, and taxed at a lower rate than other income. To learn how this would work for you, discuss your plans with a Financial Consultant.

7. Understand the extra risk involved in a leverage programme and what steps you need to take to exit a programme if it is no longer a viable option for you.

LIMITED PARTNERSHIPS

Limited Partnerships are often proposed as tax shelters. These are more complex investments and as such will not be fully discussed in this book. However, the highlights will be covered. Limited Partnerships are usually developed to take advantage of income tax breaks and must be in place by December 31st of each year.

Often high pressure tactics are used to sell Limited Partnerships especially toward the end of the year. Many people buy them for the tax break, not for the investment. Look at Limited Partnerships as an investment, just as you would any other investment. Does it make sense? Could you sell your share if you needed funds? Is there professional management of the Limited Partnership? Are there additional funds available if required by the Limited Partnership?

Also look at the assumptions in the proposal. Many people invested in Real Estate Limited Partnerships when real estate had increased in value over 10% per year for the past five years or more. Then the Real Estate market levelled out or went down so the assumptions these Limited Partnerships were based on were no longer valid. Your partnership is limited to your original investment however, if you want to save the deal, you are asked to add more money. Always look at a tax shelter first as an investment, then the tax savings are an added benefit.

No amount of tax savings will make a poor Limited Partnership a smart move.

GOING INTO BUSINESS

One way to reduce your income taxes is to set up a home based business. (See Chapter 29 for more information on how to accomplish this.)

TAX BENEFITS FOR HOME BASED BUSINESSES

Deductions for Home Based Business include:

1. You can deduct a portion of your home expenses based on the percentage related to the business.

2. Trips for business reasons are deductible - the percentage used for business only.

3. Entertaining for business reasons.

4. Equipment, furnishings, renovations and décor used exclusively for business.

5. Vehicle expenses or a percentage of your personal vehicle expense when used for business purposes can be deducted.

6. Professional development expenses when they do not qualify as education expenses.

Chapter Twenty Two

PROVIDING FOR YOUR RETIREMENT

Retirement may or may not be wonderful. It is wonderful when you use your 'golden years' to enjoy yourself, to do the things you have always wanted: to travel, to live in a sunny place in the winter, to have the hobbies you always wanted but did not have time to do.

Retirement may be difficult if you do not have the health or money to do these things. Recent surveys have shown, when people have enough money to take care of themselves, they tend to be healthier, happier, and live longer, and have more active lives. Certainly, life is enhanced by having enough money to do the things you desire.

 By managing your money early in your life, you have more fun in your retirement or your 'golden years'.

CAN YOU COUNT ON THE CANADA PENSION PLAN?

When you pay into C.P.P./Q.P.P. you expect to receive a pension from it. The question is whether or not this amount of money will cover your expenses. Remember our discussion on inflation and how it works both for and against you. Buying power is what we are talking about. A loaf of bread cost 8¢ in 1940. You can't even buy a stale loaf for 8¢ these days. Can you imagine a loaf of bread that costs $1 today costing $4? Inflation over the last 25 or 30 years has averaged 6.4% Using this average, it will take 22 years for a loaf of bread to cost $4. Every other cost will increase the same way. Take your current rent and other costs and multiply them by four to estimate your expenses 22 years from now.

What if the C.P.P./Q.P.P. payments increase at only 3.2% over the next 22 years. It does not take advanced mathematics to figure out that your pensions will NOT cover the expenses the way they have in the past.

Even in the 1990's, women still tend to be the ones to take time out from careers to have and raise children, to handle family emergencies and to look after elderly parents. These situations result in a broken career pattern which lowers current income and both government and private company pension contributions; thereby lowering the ultimate pension cheque. Add to this the fact that women tend to live at least six years longer than men and therefore, must make their pensions last longer. These are strong reasons for taking action now to secure your financial future.

GIVE YOURSELF A BREAK

One way to save for your retirement and at the same time reduce income tax is to contribute to an R.R.S.P. every year you are employed or self employed.

This tax deferral system allows your investments to accumulate tax free until withdrawn, as well as giving you a 27% to 50% tax deduction on the amount contributed each year. (See Chapter 23 for more information on R.R.S.P.'s.)

Women who believe they will be in the same or higher tax bracket at retirement as they are now, can use regular investments in ways that will increase their returns on their investments while paying little Income Tax. (See Chapter 21 on How Investments Are Taxed.)

QUESTIONS

1. How long have you contributed to C.P.P./Q.P.P. and company pension plans? What is the present value and status? If you don't know, talk to your company pension plan representative or the sponsoring company and write to Canada Pension.

2. How long must/can you contribute to a company pension plan? How is the final monthly pension payment calculated when you retire?

3. Given your estimated monthly expenses when you retire, how much income will you require?

Who is responsible for your comfortable retirement?

YOU ARE!

**Do not expect the government or your employer
to do it for you.**

Chapter Twenty Three

R.R.S.P.'S

A REGISTERED RETIREMENT SAVINGS PLAN

A Registered Retirement Savings Plan (R.R.S.P.) is **NOT** an investment. It is an Income Tax deferral system set up by the Government of Canada so you may defer tax on your current income to a later time when you redeem your R.R.S.P. and pay the tax owed. The tax you should pay on income from your high earning years is deferred to the years when theoretically, you will have less income and you will pay less Income Tax at that time.

During the time you have your R.R.S.P., your investments and the returns on these investments are sheltered from income taxes until you (or the government) decide that you must take them out of the shelter. When you deregister your R.R.S.P. you pay tax at the current rate on your total income at that time.

117

A TAX DEFERRAL SYSTEM

Under the umbrella of a tax deferral system, you may have any government approved investment included in your plan. Each separate plan must have **at least** 80% Canadian investments and up to 20% foreign investments as a percentage of the original investment. Additional money contributed to your plan must never exceed these ratios.

Once you decide to create an R.R.S.P. for yourself, there are many decisions still to be made. Should you go to a Bank, Trust Company, Credit Union, Insurance Company or a Stock Broker or Financial Consultant? Where you purchase your R.R.S.P.'s may decide what types of investments you can have. i.e. G.I.C.'S, Segregated Mutual Funds, Stocks or Bonds, or Regular Mutual Funds. Conversly, the types of Investment(s) you want may decide where you can go to obtain them.

WHEN TO START LOOKING FOR YOUR R.R.S.P.

NOW.

It doesn't matter what time of the year you are reading this book. **Now** is the time to start your search for information on which to base decisions to start your R.R.S.P.

First, gather information and talk to several people who are in a position to help you. Remember, your money is more important to you than to anyone else. Find a Financial Consultant with patience to explain exactly how this will work for you.

Secondly, compile a list of questions you want answered. There is a basic list of questions at the end of this chapter which you should expand to include questions which will help clarify the subject for you.

SPOUSAL R.R.S.P.'S

Either spouse may contribute to a Spousal R.R.S.P. The highest earner is the logical one to set up this plan. However, if one partner is going to be off work for an extended time, a Spousal Plan can take advantage of the situation. The monies in the plan will be attributed back to the contributor if withdrawn before three years have elapsed but may be withdrawn after this time virtually tax free if the spouse is still not earning income. Check with your Financial Consultant for details.

TYPES OF INVESTMENTS FOR R.R.S.P.'S

Interest Bearing Accounts are usually open (you withdraw your money at any time) and receive a low interest rate which fluctuates with the prime rate.

Guaranteed Investment Certificates (G.I.C.'s) are usually 'locked in' for a specific period of time, usually one to five years, at a set rate of interest. When interest rates are low, use the shorter term of one or two years, but when interest rates are high, invest for the longer terms for at least part of your portfolio.

Money Market Mutual Fund Accounts are based on the 90 day Treasury Bill interest rate and earn a higher rate over time than simple interest bearing accounts, but lower than the guaranteed Investment Certificate rate as a rule. These accounts are accessible and not 'locked in'.

Insurance Policy Plans are invested in Term Deposits (G.I.C.'S) or Segregated Funds. Segregated Funds are funds kept separated from the insurance company's other money. These funds are usually creditor proof.

Mutual Funds come in several forms such as Equity, Balanced, Bond, Asset Allocation, Dividend, Mortgage and Real Estate Funds, or any combination of these. The prospectus will tell you whether or not a fund qualifies for R.R.S.P.'S. If you are using a Self Directed Plan, you are also allowed to add a percentage of eligible Foreign Mutual Funds. A Self Directed Plan has more flexibility in the type of investments which can be held within it. A Financial Consultant or a Stock Broker will set one up for you.

Bonds are long term debt sold by companies, utilities and governments (local, provincial, and federal) on which they pay a prescribed rate of interest until maturity. When a Bond pays higher interest than you currently receive for a debt instrument, they sell for a premium which results in a higher return. If a Bond pays lower interest than you can obtain currently, they are discounted and your return is lower. They may be added to your R.R.S.P. if they are Canadian or within the 20% foreign content.

Stocks are shares of a company which pay Dividends or have an increase in value which is a Capital Gain. Many Stocks are listed on the major Stock Exchanges in Canada and are eligible for your R.R.S.P. There are special regulations for stocks in companies which are not listed on the Stock Exchanges in Canada.

*NOTE: The section on 'Types of Investments' was previously discussed in Chapter 8. The types of investments are the same, whether or not they are part of your R.R.S.P.

HOW MANY R.R.S.P.'S CAN YOU HAVE?

You may have as many R.R.S.P.'s as you want to buy, but you should have only as many as you can understand and 'track'. Usually, this means one or two plans. Some plans allow you to include several different types of investments within them. Other plans allow only one type of investment.

WHY YOU MIGHT HAVE MORE THAN ONE PLAN

You start your R.R.S.P. at 20 years of age and you deposit it into a bank R.R.S.P. for five years. When you are 25, perhaps the interest rates go to 11% so you lock your plan into a five year Guaranteed Investment Certificate. For three years while the interest rates are high you start a new plan each year which is invested for five years. Then the interest rates go down to just over 5%, so you look for another investment which will give you a higher rate of return.

According to our count you have five different R.R.S.P.'s. You cannot move the G.I.C.'s into the new R.R.S.P. account since they still have one to four years to run until maturity. If you continue to start new R.R.S.P.'s every time you change tactics, you will soon have a challenge to keep track of everything. As each G.I.C. matures you can transfer the money into a different investment or consolidate several into one or two plans. You could set up one plan which includes Canadian Mutual Funds, a Money Market Fund, and a Foreign Mutual Fund component.

You should maximize the returns on your investments but you also need to be able to access some or all of the money during an emergency. Keeping a portion of your R.R.S.P. in a Money Market account within a self directed R.R.S.P. would provide for emergencies. Any amount withdrawn from your R.R.S.P. must be added to your income.

ROLL OVERS

You can 'Roll Over' any R.R.S.P. from one investment into another investment as long as it is available. You usually can not move a G.I.C. Investment until it's maturity date. You must comply with the Financial Institutions regulations about notice and any payments needed to close or transfer an account. Your Financial Consultant will use a government form called a T2033. This transfers the money from one account to the new account without ever coming into your hands, so it has no Income Tax implications.

Using the government form T2033 allows you to change Financial Institutions, Agents, Brokers or Representatives without coming into possession of the funds or incurring any Income Tax.

LOCKED IN PLANS

'Locked in' plans may be 'Rolled Over' but only into another 'Locked In' plan. Some plans will not allow you to move the money until they are paid out by the plan.

'Locked In' plans can be 'Rolled Over' but withdrawals can not begin until you are age 55 to 65 depending on the type of pension or 'Locked In' R.R.S.P.

ASKING QUESTIONS

Sometimes it is not easy to ask questions, but the future this money will provide for is yours. It is your right to understand the plans, the restrictions, and the options you have. If you don't understand, ask more questions. When explanations do not make sense to you, find another consultant who can clearly explain in words, diagrams, or examples. It may mean the difference between being able to take enjoyable holidays when you retire or having to scrimp on your grocery bill each week.

CHARGES AND COSTS

Many public Financial Institutions do not charge fees up front, others do have charges. Some plans charge fees when you withdraw all or part of the monies, or redeem it within a certain period of time after starting the plan. Ask what the charges are and how often they will be deducted. Independent Financial Consultants are paid by commission only for their knowledge and advice. Some charges are reasonable, and you should know what they are and when they will occur.

QUESTIONS TO ASK

1. Are there fees when I withdraw all or part of my R.R.S.P.?

2. Does my Investment have a 'Locked In' term during which I cannot transfer it?

3. What type of investment is this?

4. What are the risk factors and diversification of this investment?

Chapter Twenty Four

ESTIMATING FINANCIAL NEEDS AT RETIREMENT

How can you attain enough income to give yourself a comfortable retirement? It depends on several things. What does 'comfortable' mean to you? At your present age, how much discretionary income do you have in the years between now and your retirement? Are you eligible for private, Company or Government Pension plans, or Old Age Security payments when you retire? Information on some of these are easy to obtain, while others must be estimates.

More complex issues include your present and future health, where you choose to live, the lifestyle you desire, as well as hobbies and travel plans. Factor inflation in and you end up with a challenge for you and your calculator. You cannot plan for all contingencies.

Miller's Law: "Unless you put your money to work for you, you will work for your money."

A simple way to project your retirement needs is to ask yourself the question, "Will I need more or less income than I am living on presently?" You may have lower fixed expenses because you have paid for your home, and certain other expenses may have been reduced or eliminated. However, you may have higher expenses because you want to live in a warm climate during our Canadian winter or you may travel more, or have increased entertainment expenses because you never had time to entertain while you were working.

WHAT IS YOUR IDEAL LIFESTYLE?

Think about what you would like to do; how you would like to live. Make this a realistic vision and not one based on winning a lottery! Estimate your costs as more or less than you are spending now on living expenses. Would it cost you 10% more/less; 20% more/less, to live as you would like?

INVESTMENTS PROVIDE ADDITIONAL INCOME FOR YOUR RETIREMENT

Investment Consultants usually recommend that you withdraw no more than 1% per month from your investments. If you have Mutual Funds or a **Registered Retirement Income Fund (R.R.I.F)**, this is easy to accomplish. A 1% per month withdrawal on a $100,000 investment is $1,000. At this rate your investment **should** keep the Capital intact and possibly even increase it. When the market goes down, you can help to preserve your Capital if you decrease your monthly withdrawal amount. Talk to your Financial Consultant 'in depth' about how this will work for you.

WITHDRAWING YOUR R.R.S.P.

You must withdraw/convert your R.R.S.P. by the end of the year in which you turn 71. You may withdraw all or part anytime (as long as the investment itself is available).

Upon withdrawal there is a percentage WITHHELD by the Financial Institution and sent to Revenue Canada as a contribution toward your income taxes. This amount is added to all your other contributions and your taxes are deducted from it. The deduction from your withdrawal **is not a tax** on the R.R.S.P.

The cash value of the withdrawal is added to your income when your taxes are computed, then the tax bill is calculated on your total income. If your income is low (including your R.R.S.P. withdrawal) you are taxed at a low rate. If your income, including the R.R.S.P. is high, you are taxed at a higher rate. The amount withheld at the redemption of your R.R.S.P. has no relation to the actual Income Tax you will pay.

R.R.S.P. REVIEW

WHAT THEY ARE:

1. An R.R.S.P. is a *tax deferral system* set up by the Government of Canada and administered by trustees.

2. They shelter your money from taxation until you need or want to redeem it. When you turn age 71, you are required by law to start withdrawing at least a minimum each year.

3. R.R.S.P.'s are taxable **ONLY** as part of your income in the year of withdrawal.

4. Each plan may have between 80% and 100% Canadian content and from 0% to 20% Foreign content.

WHAT THEY ARE NOT:

1. An R.R.S.P. is not a tax shelter. A tax shelter means you never have to pay taxes on your investment.

2. An Investment. It is a mechanism for deferring your taxes on this investment.

3. The investments within your R.R.S.P. are not necessarily 'safe'. The security depends upon which of many eligible investments you place your money in; the credibility of the managers; the risk inherent in the particular investment; and other factors which are the same as any other investment you make.

4. The Investments themselves are not run, or supervised by the Government or the Trustees. The Government and Trustees supervise the plan. This supervision consists of making sure the investments within the plan qualify as to Canadian content; the mechanisms for depositing and withdrawing the money; the withholding tax amount; and issuing the proper tax receipts.

Chapter Twenty Five

INVESTMENT STRATEGIES

- **PLAN I:** Do nothing.
- **PLAN II:** Ask a lot of questions and then do nothing. At least you will talk a good game.
- **PLAN III:** Do whatever the last person you talked to suggested and blame them if it does not work.
- **PLAN IV:** All of the above.
- **PLAN V:** Decide you are the person most concerned with your financial welfare and take charge. Ask questions, understand the concepts, make choices, diversify, keep all extra dollars away from the taxman.

WORK YOUR PLAN

When you have looked at the other plans and decided that Plan V is the only one that will help you obtain your objectives, you can start – **you already have** – by reading this book and implementing the savings and investment strategies that apply to your situation.

You need to read each section carefully and do the exercises where applicable. Keep your copy of this book handy. When you see your Insurance Agent, make new investments or renew a mortgage, use the question sections to help you make informed decisions. Remember to ask questions in any area you do not understand. Write the answers in this book. It is very easy to get home after an intensive session with a Financial Consultant not remembering what was said in answer to certain questions. Do not be afraid to call back at any time to ask further questions.

Listing what you have, asking questions and understanding how your current investments work is a great beginning. Your future goals are an exciting journey upon which you have just launched yourself.

Two factors in Plan V have not been addressed so far in this text. They are:
1. Risk Tolerance.
2. Continuous Refinement.

UNDERSTANDING YOUR RISK TOLERANCE

There is risk in managing your money. There is a risk in doing nothing. There is a risk that something you do may not ultimately be the best decision. Given these risks, many people feel that doing nothing is preferable – at least you do not lose your money.

In fact, the reverse is true. Do something because to do nothing is riskier. Minimize risk by **diversifing** your money into different types of investments. The investments you choose depends on you, your ability to understand the investments, and how you view diversification.

There are 'rules of thumb' about how much money a woman of a certain age should invest into Interest, Bonds, Stocks or Mutual Funds. 'Rules of thumb' are only **guidelines** and should be viewed as such. If you are a person who needs to increase your return because you did not start your investment program until later in life, you may need to make more aggressive plans.

CONTINUOUS REFINEMENT

The most carefully laid plans need adjustment when events change your life, the stock market fluctuates, or a recession occurs.

If you were a pilot who has just taken off from Vancouver flying to Hawaii, there are a multitude of small adjustments to make. When a storm or malfunction occurs, there are bigger adjustments to make. The pilot does not say – "We set the direction and did everything right. We do not need to pay attention to any new information from the Air Traffic Controller or other signals." The pilot would quickly be in real difficulty and end up missing Hawaii completely.

This is the same kind of result many people experience once they have made one poor financial decision and decide not to make any more decisions at all. Your financial plan is subject to the same necessity for refinement.

FIVE STEPS TO ENHANCE
YOUR FINANCIAL FUTURE

1. Set the goals for your financial future by using specific amounts of money. Visualize yourself attaining these goals. Do not let negative thinking get in your way.

2. Decide the actions you will take to attain these goals, the time frames, and what percentages you are currently comfortable with for each type of investment you intend to make. There are no absolutes here.

3. Decide how often you will complete a financial 'check up' on your progress. Do this at least once or twice per year.

4. Make adjustments as required when any changes occur in your life, the economy, the markets, or your goals. Yes, you can change your goals.

Example
If the stock market tumbles, you may wish to purchase more Stocks or Mutual Funds, instead of selling as many people do. Buy more when others are selling. This is the ultimate '10%, 20% or 30% off' sale.

---

5. Continue until you attain your financial goals. Watch a child learning to walk. They do not usually go from crawling to walking without some falls. They just get up and start over again.

Chapter
Twenty Six

SAVING FOR EDUCATION

One of the most important financial obligations you may have is to save for your child's or your own education. There are several ways to shelter the returns on your investments and thereby increase the money available for educational purposes. You may be able to finance all education through your personal income and savings. A formal Registered Education Savings Plan (R.E.S.P.) helps you save some tax.

A TAX SHELTER FOR EDUCATION

When you set up a Registered Educational Savings Plan, the capital you contribute does not incur a tax deduction. The returns on the investment **are** sheltered within the plan and are allowed to grow tax free.

Only the returns are taxed when the beneficiary withdraws the money for educational purposes. They are taxed in the hands of the student when withdrawn to pay for full time post-secondary education expenses. The student's tax rate should be lower than the contributor's.

The tax is thereby deferred and usually reduced or eliminated. The contributor has the right to remove the principal from most plans without tax or penalty at any time. Be wary if the plan you are discussing does not have this option.

All growth earned within a registered plan **MUST** be used to pay for post-secondary educational expenses or is taxed in the hands of the contributor. Contributions currently are restricted to $1,500 per year to a maximum of $31,500. One or more contributors can pay into a plan, but there must be only one plan per child.

There are no restrictions on the amount of 'foreign' investments that can be held in an R.E.S.P.

An R.E.S.P. may be in existence for a maximum of 21 years by law, and any growth not used by the end of that time must be donated to an educational institution.

TYPES OF PLANS

MUTUAL FUND
SELF DIRECTED PLANS

A Self Directed Plan means YOU select the Mutual Funds for your R.E.S.P. There are over 500 Mutual Funds that are eligible. Plans include monthly or yearly contributions with minimum deposits of $50, small enrolment and annual charges. Any number of beneficiaries can be named per plan including yourself or other adults, with no age restrictions. The plan may exist for up to 21 years. These plans are available for all post-secondary academic education, including post graduate study.

Unused Funds will be designated to set up a scholarship, or as a grant to a post-secondary institution.

SECURITY FIRM PLAN

A minimum of $10,000 is recommended to open a self directed plan so the principal must be transferred from another plan. Investments are selected by the investor with a broker's recommendation.

There are no age or academic restrictions and may include any number of beneficiaries. The plan may exist for up to 21 years. There is usually a $100 annual administration fee and a small cost to close the plan.

INSURANCE COMPANY PLAN

This plan is usually a Universal Life Policy which is based on insuring the child's life using extra premiums to finance the scholarship. This policy will pay out in 20 years. This is a type of endowment policy.

Monthly or lump sum additions can be made to these plans. There can be any number of beneficiaries for a plan and they can be changed at any time.

There is no enrolment fee.

The contributor has a choice of an income or equity portfolio. There are no age or academic restrictions.

UNIVERSITY SCHOLARSHIP PLANS

Regular monthly or yearly contributions to the plan vary according to the age of the beneficiary and the amount of money per payment.

All money is pooled and the plan invests in fixed income type securities. All **successful** students share from the total pool of funds.

Enrolment fee plus an annual administration fee is charged.

A child must not be older than 10 or 12 years (depending on the plan) to be enrolled. The funds from the plan are only used to cover the 2nd, 3rd, and 4th year of post-secondary education for **qualifying** students.

To qualify, the beneficiary must meet set academic requirements to continue in the plan.

There is only one beneficiary per plan. However the beneficiary can be changed while the child is under thirteen or under some specific conditions. All **interest** is lost if the child does not pursue a post-secondary education.

If the beneficiary does not continue post-secondary education, all returns on the investment continue in the plan for the benefit of the beneficiaries of the company's other plans.

Any remaining principal is returned to the contributor.

Chapter Twenty Seven

SELECTING PROFESSIONALS

We use mechanics, dentists, doctors, chiropractors and lawyers to help us with many things where we have little or no experience. We should use financial professionals in the financial areas of our lives. Financial Consultants make things easier and have specialized knowledge in investments, credit and income tax which would take us a lot of time, energy, and money to learn.

However, certain qualities and characteristics make some professionals better at helping women.

QUALITIES

A professional should be service oriented, open to questions, and give clear answers. All costs should be explained to you. A professional would not ask you to do anything on a 'just trust me' basis and should never ask you to sign papers without reviewing them.

DOCTORS, DENTISTS, AND
OTHER HEALTH CARE PERSONNEL

Your health is your concern and you are paying for the information, help and directions that you obtain from any health care professional. You should focus on good health and how you personally can achieve this goal. Health care professionals who do not answer your questions, recommend a second (or third) opinion for major surgery or treatment, are not of the quality you deserve. Your health is your responsibility!

LAWYERS

Ask your friends for referrals when looking for a lawyer. Most of us do not use a lawyer very often. A lawyer should be service oriented and willing to answer your questions.

Most lawyers allow a complimentary initial interview. Write a list of questions regarding the fee schedule and how they are to be paid.

REAL ESTATE AGENTS

Professional Representatives or Brokers sell homes no matter what the real estate 'market' is doing. They will do a market evaluation for no charge and will tell you what you need to know about the market, your home/property, and the average length of time it takes to sell. They will also discuss what you really NEED to do to your home to make it more marketable and what improvements would give you a good return on your investment.

Real Estate Representatives will answer your questions openly and not hide facts which you may not want to hear. They will also give you a list of 'comparables' - homes which have sold recently and are similar to yours. This will show you how they arrived at the listing price. Discuss your home with several realtors and ask them questions. This will assist you to make the best choice.

BUYING A HOME

When buying a home, a successful Real Estate Sales Representative will ask you questions about the area in which you want to live, the price you want to pay, lifestyle, number of bedrooms, your family, and whether you want such things as a fireplace, pool, main level laundry room and the number of bathrooms.

The Representative may even ask you what your favourite colours are, the style of your furniture and what type of entertaining you usually do.

You should ask for a list of satisfied customers who have bought or sold through the agent.

THE CONTRACT

Many Representatives or Brokers will ask you to sign a 90 day contract because they need the time to promote your home through the paper and other agents. You may break this contract if there is not enough action. Action means advertising, people going through your home, such as potential buyers, open houses, other real estate agents, and your agent's activity. You should try for a shorter contract, since you will see more action in a short time.

In a competitive market you can also negotiate a lower percentage for the fee with some Real Estate Representatives.

You also need to decide whether or not you want your home to be listed with a Multiple Listing Agency (M.L.S.). There are many companies, besides the company you chose, listed with this service and all these Representatives have the opportunity to sell your home. This usually costs an additional 1% but may mean a faster sale .

LIFE INSURANCE AGENTS

Life Insurance Agents should not use fear to sell you policies more costly than you really need. All policies have both 'pros and cons'. The Agent should know and explain the negatives as well as the positives of any policy.

The Agent should have access to a variety of companies so they can quote the least expensive policy that is right for you.

Do not be overwhelmed by the name of the policy but find out what type of policy is being discussed. Is the policy a Whole Life , a Universal Life or Term? (Refer to Chapter 18 to review the overall conditions of each type of policy.)

BENEFICIARIES

The beneficiaries should be named specifically in each of your insurance policies. Unpaid expenses or bills remaining after you die will not be covered by the proceeds of the insurance policy. Your beneficiaries will receive the full amount of the policy and your liabilities will come out of the estate. If the estate does not have enough money to cover these expenses, they cannot come out of the money from the insurance policies. You may take out a separate policy for this purpose if you want to be sure such expenses are covered.

REVOCABLE OR IRREVOCABLE BENEFICIARY

A revocable beneficiary means that the owner or life insured can change the beneficiary at will. However, an irrevocable beneficiary means the owner or life insured cannot change the beneficiary without the written consent of the beneficiary already named. Irrevocable beneficiaries are often used in divorce settlements.

REMEMBER: Never have 'estate' as your beneficiary, unless you have no specific people who you wish to give your assets. To creditor proof your policy, you must name a person/persons as the beneficiary(ies).

ACCOUNTANTS

You may require a tax consultant or someone to look after all your accounts. Obtain references from friends or colleagues when searching for an accountant.

FINANCIAL CONSULTANTS

A Financial Consultant is one professional most people require. Shop around for someone you feel comfortable to talk to and ask questions. Choose someone who gives you answers which you fully understand.

You want a Financial Consultant who keeps in touch, whether by personal interview, phone call, letter, newsletter, and most of all, by reports on how your investments are doing. They also do not ask you to go into a risky venture with all your money or to put 'all your eggs in one basket'!

WHAT TO LOOK FOR
A competent Financial Consultant will:

1. Treat you and your wishes with respect.

2. Clearly answer your questions.

3. Explain all terms to you.

4. Discuss the fees and expenses of your plans.

5. Give you excellent service.

DON'T SETTLE FOR ANYTHING LESS!

"How may I help you?"

Chapter Twenty Eight

THE SUDDENLY SINGLE SYNDROME

Single again! The single state may come about by reason of bereavement, divorce or separation. The choice is not always yours but future decisions will be. When you have had a relationship and it ends suddenly or slowly, there is often a period of time when you must make or remake decisions under pressure or emotional trauma – decisions which will affect the rest of your life. Take your time and get as much information as possible before making lifestyle changes or putting your money in an inaccessible place.

WILLS

Rewrite your Will when changes happen in your life, your relationships, or your lifestyle. Make sure your estate goes where you wish. Emotional times make it difficult to make decisions. You may be able to change your Will or add a codicil to bring it into line.

THE EXECUTOR OF YOUR ESTATE

Executors/Executrixes need to be named and it is wise to name at least two who understand your wishes. Discuss your wishes with them. If there are children involved, be certain the guardians named are willing to handle the task and are not the executors. This keeps the money separate from the people who will be spending it.

IMPORTANT SKILLS OF YOUR EXECUTOR

Your Executors/Executrixes should have some knowledge and ability in money management, taxes, and investments. You may name a Financial Institution as the Executor. The positive aspect is they are always there. The negative side is your beneficiaries may deal with people other than those with whom you made arrangements.

Anyone who has assets, and has someone they wish cared for, should have a Will and review it yearly.

DIVIDING YOUR ESTATE

You may use percentages to guarantee an equitable split of your assets. If you want to leave money to charities and are not sure how large your estate will be when the Will is put into effect, use 5% of your estate up to a maximum of $5,000.

INSURANCE POLICIES

Check your insurance policies to be certain you have correctly named your beneficiaries and your ex-partner's name is removed. Your Insurance Agent has the forms for this.

Your responsibilities may have changed. You should review your life insurance policies. You may be the sole provider for your family and as such may require additional insurance. Or, you may no longer have as many responsibilities and be able to reduce your insurance policies.

LIVING OR FAMILY TRUSTS

One way to ensure that your children or other family members receive your estate is to set up a living or family trust.

It is almost impossible to retrieve assets which have been given away, when the care you receive is not what you want. Money spent or lost in poor investments can not be spent on your care.

 There is a danger of giving assets (money, investments, art, jewellery) to children or other family members before you die in return for their 'looking after' you.

Keep control of your own money.

Chapter Twenty Nine

GOING INTO BUSINESS

The trend of the 90's includes more jobs being created by small businesses and more women going into business for themselves. Over 60% of new small businesses are started by women and more than 80% of these are successful.

THE BENEFITS FOR YOU

1. You work for yourself and have control of your destiny.

2. You can focus on your strengths and hire people to do those things in which you are not as competent as you would like.

3. You can be service oriented.

4. You can help others by hiring and training them.

5. You are able to start a small business in your home and have low overhead.

6. You may save on your income tax.

HOW TO START

Complete a thorough market study and business plan. Obtain accurate cost estimates and then increase them by 30%. Estimate sales and then decrease them by 30%; always round 'up' for expenses and 'down' for income.

Be sure you are willing to work the long hours required for a full time business, or decide the number of hours per day you are going to devote to your part-time business.

YOUR BUSINESS GOALS

Write out your goals, financial and personal as well as your business plan. Decide the size you intend your company to be in five years. You will be surprised at how much easier some business decisions will be once you know these basics.

You are allowed to deduct home and vehicle expenses from business income within government guidelines. Conferences, travel and entertainment expenses (80% of **your** meals) which relate to the business are deductions. All expenses must be for the benefit of the business. For instance, you are able to deduct accounting, marketing, management, and employee relation courses. A course on painting techniques would not be an expense unless it was business related. Going into business is a great way to learn new skills, use your current skills and have more flexibility. If your business does not prosper, take your new skills to a new career.

GOVERNMENT INCENTIVES

Check out the current government incentives such as venture capital loans, research grants and job training incentives. Some of these may be of help to you, but remember – there are usually strings attached, records to keep and reports to make. Some programmes have restrictions on them if you have not been in business for more than six months or one year. It takes time to research these programmes but they are worth the effort if they help you establish a business in which you will be successful.

FINANCING

Financing a small business may be one of your first and most important endeavours. The easiest way is through personal savings or income, then loans from family or friends. Treat family and friends as REAL investors; show them hard copies of your written plans.

Go to Financial Institutions such as Banks, Trust Companies and Credit Unions if you do not have the resources to privately finance your business.

Be sure to take clear copies of all your plans, income projections, profit and loss projections, marketing plans and feasibility studies as well as a résumé or qualifications.

CAREFULLY CHOOSE YOUR BANKER

Women often have more of a challenge obtaining both collateral and operating loans for business. When loans are granted, more collateral may be required for the institution's security.

OBTAINING CREDIT

Traditional women's businesses have enough difficulty; non traditional businesses may require more than twice the amount of collateral for security on a loan.

You may be asked to have a co-signer for your loans. This is becoming the accepted practice for many new businesses started by both men and women.

A LINE OF CREDIT

A line of credit is very important for a new small business for well-rounded overall financing. Be prepared for more resistance from a lender and counter the resistance by well researched, well documented and professional looking plans.

PROFESSIONAL PROPOSALS

Have someone else check your plans and documents before you show them to a financial institution. Be certain there are no spelling or mathematical errors.

Have a cover page that names the business, date of your plan, your name, address and phone number. If you have a word processor which has different type sizes, make the name of your company big and bold.

YOUR PROPOSAL SHOULD INCLUDE

Market Study - The need for your product or service. When completed it should include the number of surveys evaluated, statistical analysis, other studies and quotes.

Background Information - The skills you have, and why you will be able to manage this business.

Description of the product or service you plan to offer and the selling price. Include anything special about your product. Describe your competition and why your product or service is better, less expensive or easier to use. Highlight any contracts already in place or pre-sold products. Note any contracts you have to purchase your stock or materials at set prices.

Business Plan which includes cash flow projections for at least three years, income statements based on these, and profit and loss statements.

Expansion projections and their timing should be included if they are part of your plans.

Complete the entire exercise because **you need to know** the numbers and dollars involved and so do your financial backers. This will show whether or not it will be a profitable business and how soon the business would show a profit. If you believe you will be successful after you have analyzed your plans, then you will be able to use these plans to obtain financing.

ABOUT LENDERS

Lenders have the interest of their institution first in their minds. Many financial institutions have been divested of funds by people with less than perfect integrity in recent years, and therefore are more wary. There is no easy access to money. When a financial institution grants you credit or loans, they may want signed documents which are not in your best interest to give them. If you want the money you may have to do this anyway.

PERSONAL GUARANTEES

Personal guarantees are foremost among documents for which you may be asked. If you decide to sign, immediately ask what conditions will have to be met before you can take back your personal guarantee. As soon as the conditions are met, retrieve these papers. Otherwise you may never get them back and they will still held as security.

SHOULD YOU INCORPORATE

You can start a small business in your own name and there is no need to incorporate or even register it. You and your business are the same under the law, your assets are the same and the income tax paid is the same.

When you want to operate under a business name, you must at least register your company. It may be a sole proprietorship or a partnership (with one or more partners). The company is still tied to you; the responsibilities, income taxes, and liabilities, are all yours (and your partners). To obtain the registration papers, you need to contact your Provincial Ministry of Corporate Affairs.

It is usually easier to handle a business that grosses less than $30,000 a year as a sole proprietorship or partnership. Remember, you must adhere to all legislation, pay P.S.T./G.S.T. and follow local rules about home based businesses.

An incorporation can be either Provincial or Federal. A corporation is an entity by itself. If something happens to you, the company continues. When your business is not incorporated and you die, the business does not continue. A lawyer is needed to incorporate your business.

QUESTIONS TO ASK BEFORE GOING INTO BUSINESS FOR YOURSELF

1. Am I willing to work harder than a 9:00 - 5:00 job?

2. Do I consider myself a risk taker? Can I reduce risks by looking realistically at situations and analyzing them to arrive at solid answers, even if I am part of the problem?

3. Am I flexible, and do I have a variety of skills?

Chapter Thirty

GOOSE BUMPS AND OTHER SCARY THINGS

This chapter is a collection of diverse information that was recommended to the author during the writing of this book. It does not include everything, since the decision was made to limit the book's size for easy handling. Many additional topics will be discussed in the next book *Financial Strategies for Women: The Second Step*, and in the audio tapes *Financial Strategies for Women: The Basics*. (To order, use the form in the back of the book).

TIME SHARES

Vacation properties are wonderful and one of the problems has always been their maintenance. Time sharing seems to be the way to go and certainly the marketing is energetic, creative and full of subliminal pressures and high pressure selling techniques. Look at the pros and cons of putting $10,000, $12,000, $15,000 or more into a Time Share.

A Time Share gives you a great vacation spot. You can usually exchange time for other areas you would like to visit and if you cannot make it one year, you can rent your spot to someone else.

However, you must still travel to your vacation paradise at your own expense, buy your own food and pay for entertainment. Your vacation will still cost you a considerable amount. Add to this your yearly maintenance fees and you have spent a lot of money.

AN ALTERNATIVE

Invest your capital in a way which produces at least a 10% return. If your original investment was $15,000, this would give you $1,500 each year towards your vacation expenses. Add to this any amounts you would save by not buying a time share – the maintenance fees, extra travel costs, especially if your time share is Hawaii! Then take your vacation wherever you want, whenever you want.

If you do look at a Time Share proposition, take a few days and have a lawyer look over the contracts. Think about what you really want to do, away from the hype of the sales centre.

POWER OF ATTORNEY

A Power of Attorney is a very powerful legal document. When in force, it gives total rights to the person named to look after and control all monies or a specific portion of the monies for the person who grants the Power of Attorney. This can also be granted through the Courts. If the person named dies, the Power of Attorney is cancelled.

This document is often used to help older parents with decision making, paying bills and business affairs when the parent becomes incapable of handling these matters.

Never give a Power of Attorney to anyone whom you do not completely trust. It is very difficult – almost impossible – to retrieve your assets when they have been spent or lost by someone with a Power of Attorney who moved your money without your approval. This leaves you powerless to act on your own behalf.

A Power of Attorney could be requested by a Stock Broker or Financial Consultant to handle your account. The result is that they may change your investments without your knowledge or permission.

DO NOT SIGN A POWER OF ATTORNEY unless you also have **IN WRITING** exactly the circumstances in which it will be used.

CO-SIGNING A LOAN

Co-signing a loan for anyone, even for a husband or child creates a legal obligation. If the person you co-signed for fails to pay, the payments are your responsibility. When you do co-sign, you need to have a legitimate way to be sure the payments are being made.

MARKET DOWNTURNS

The Stock Market and the Real Estate Market both go up and down in accordance with what is happening to the economy of the country, or the area where the investment is located, trends, or fads. Many investments are based on projections from these trends and a projection is still just an assumption. Both types of investments may give you extremely rewarding results but you do need to be aware of the total picture.

Find uninvolved experts to give you an opinion and pay them for their advice. A small amount of money paid for a professional opinion before you invest could save you thousands.

NEGATIVE PRESS

The media sometimes scares people into moves which are not in their best interest. When you develop your plan you should stick to it unless you have solid information on which to change your decisions.

PRESSURE SALES

When buying anything you should be given the opportunity to think about your decision. Do not allow someone to pressure you into buying by saying: *"The offer will not be available if you do not take it NOW!"* or *"The price is going up, I can't guarantee you will get it for this price"* Tell the salesperson: *"I'll get back to you, I want to think about this"*

If you are not entirely certain of your choice, 'sleep on it'. A quality retailer or salesperson will give you this opportunity. Ask for the salesperson's card in order that the sale will be credited to him/her. On door to door purchases, you have 48 hours to change your mind.

Beware of the 'no interest, no payment until later' plans. Read the contract. In some instances you may be required to pay all the accumulated interest if you do not pay your entire bill by the due date. The interest charged is often 2% to 2.5% a month or 24% to 30% a year.

Conclusion

CONGRATULATIONS

You have taken a very positive step in making your financial future more secure. You have researched information which will save you money, increase your credit worthiness and increase the return on your investments.

There are only two ways to have more money to invest for your future:
- Earn more income.
- Reduce your expenses.

Paul Rockel, President of the Regal Capital Group, says, "There are only three ways to make money:
1. People at work.
2. Money at work.
3. Win a lottery.

Since the odds of number three happening are probably more than a million to one and cannot be recommended as a sound financial plan; let's concentrate on numbers one and two."

It is up to you which you choose, but would you rather work because you want to, not because you must. That leaves us with number two or *money at work*. You can conserve the money you earn and make it work FOR you.

Rid yourself of the lingering notion that someone will always be there to look after you. Then, if someone never comes along, or the one you are with now, leaves, you will not be left 'high and dry'. If you find someone with whom you would like to share your life, you can plan your financial futures together.

This book lays the groundwork for many exciting ways for you to increase your knowledge of how money works in our society and how you can make it work harder for you!

In the first chapter, you were encouraged to become a detective who was investigating a case, searching for clues and information. You have graduated to Junior Detective, First Class. It wasn't difficult, was it? Fifteen or twenty minutes of reading per day should be a habit by now. The good news is that there is much more to learn. Remember, you are the one most concerned with your finances.

 No one else will watch over your financial future as well as you do.

WHERE TO GO FROM HERE

The next step is learning more ways of increasing your knowledge. By becoming more competent, you will be able to make informed decisions while feeling confident you are able to handle the results. The Financial Post,

The Financial Times, The Globe & Mail business section are good sources of investment information.

 Continue to study and practice what you learn. Decisions will become easier with practice. Set goals as guidelines.

Write down your plans. Revise them regularly. All the plans in the world are of no value if you do not *TAKE ACTION* and revise them on a regular basis. Do you remember the flight to Hawaii?

Women sometimes say they are not interested in money; they care more for people. You are more able to care for others as well as yourself, when you have sufficient security so you do not have to worry.

Our brain is like a clothes closet. Some closets have lots of hooks for clothes; others, not very many. Some people do not have *hooks* in their brain to hold financial information. All you need to do is install a few hooks and the information will have a place to hang. Why not install many hooks and keep on adding. The more hooks you have, the more room you have for additional information. There is lots to learn!

**Managing your money is the ultimate
'Do It Yourself' Project.**

Read any chapters you are not comfortable with again. Keep your financial information handy. Use the questions in the chapters, plus your own questions, when you talk to professionals.

Complete all the information in the Personal Financial Review (P.F.R.) in the back of the book. Use the offer W.I.N. has given you of a complimentary analysis of your financial status as described on page 4.

It is your money. Use it. Make it work for you - after all, you have earned it!

Create the opportunity to learn more – watch for the forthcoming tapes and books.

RID YOURSELF OF THE LINGERING NOTION THAT SOMEONE WILL ALWAYS BE THERE TO LOOK AFTER YOU.

MY PERSONAL FINANCIAL STRATEGIES

I have:
- asked more questions _____
- reduced expenses _____
- increased returns on my investments _____

I intend to:
- learn more _____
- clear or reduce credit card balances _____
- use credit wisely _____
- learn new job skills _____
- start my own business _____
- reduce income taxes by contributing to R.R.S.P.'S _____

NOTES

This book was in the process of being printed when speculation escalated that the budget of February 1994 would bring changes in the Income Tax Act affecting the current lifetime Capital Gains Exemption of $100,000 (as per examples on pages 54 and 108) and probably reduce the R.R.S.P. contribution levels. These, as well as any additional changes, underline the need to constantly update your financial strategies to reflect the latest tax laws. A plan which is very advantageous one year may be detrimental the next year. The need to be up-to-date on all changes highlights the need to work with knowledgeable Financial Advisors.

NOTES

NOTES

NOTES

NOTES

GOAL SETTING GUIDE

MY PERSONAL GOALS ARE: **I WILL NEED**

1._____ $ _____
2._____ $ _____
3._____ $ _____
4._____ $ _____
TOTAL $ _____

MY FAMILY GOALS ARE: **I WILL NEED**

1._____ $ _____
2._____ $ _____
3._____ $ _____
4._____ $ _____
TOTAL $ _____

MY FINANCIAL GOALS ARE: **I WILL NEED**

1._____ $ _____
2._____ $ _____
3._____ $ _____
4._____ $ _____
TOTAL $ _____

SHORT TERM GOALS   **I WILL NEED**

Daily Interest Savings $ _____
Canada Savings Bonds $ _____
Money Market Fund $ _____
Separate Savings $ _____
TOTAL $ _____

MEDIUM TERM GOALS   **I WILL NEED**

1._____ $ _____
2._____ $ _____
3._____ $ _____
4._____ $ _____
TOTAL $ _____

LONG TERM GOALS   **I WILL NEED**

1._____ $ _____
2._____ $ _____
3._____ $ _____
4._____ $ _____
TOTAL $ _____

NET WORTH STATEMENT

ASSETS

BANK
- Chequing Account(s) $_____
- Savings Account(s) $_____
- G.I.C.'s $_____
- Term Deposits $_____

BONDS
- Canada Savings Bonds $_____
- Other Bonds $_____

BUSINESS INVESTMENTS $_____

LIFE INSURANCE
- Cash Surrender Value $_____

MONEY OWED TO ME
- Mortgages $_____
- Notes $_____

MUTUAL FUNDS
- Regular $_____
- Segregated $_____

STOCKS $_____

R.R.S.P.'S
- Bank $_____
- Insurance $_____
- Mutual Funds $_____
- Stocks $_____

VACATION PROPERTY $_____

ART or ANTIQUES $_____

COINS or COLLECTIBLES $_____

EQUIPMENT
- Camera, Computer, Hobby $_____

JEWELLERY - Personal, Heirlooms $_____

VEHICLE(S) $_____

MISCELLANEOUS $_____

TOTAL ASSETS   _$_____

NET WORTH STATEMENT

LIABILITIES

ACCOUNTS PAYABLE	$ _____
BUSINESS LOANS	$ _____
CREDIT CARDS	
- _____	$ _____
- _____	$ _____
- _____	$ _____
- _____	$ _____
- _____	$ _____
- _____	$ _____
- _____	$ _____
CAR LOAN(S)	$ _____
FURNITURE OR APPLIANCE LOANS	$ _____
HOUSE MORTGAGE	$ _____
INCOME OR PROPERTY TAXES	$ _____
PERSONAL LOAN(S)	$ _____
VACATION LOAN(S)	$ _____
VACATION PROPERTY LOAN(S)	$ _____
OTHER MONIES OWED	$ _____
	$ _____
TOTAL LIABILITIES	$ _____

SUMMARY

TOTAL ASSETS	$ _____
DEDUCT LIABILITIES	
YOUR CURRENT NET WORTH	$ _____

CASH FLOW STATEMENT

INCOME

EMPLOYMENT
- Wages $_____
- Commissions $_____
- Contracts $_____
- Bonuses $_____

CHILD
- Child tax credit $_____

ALIMONY $_____

CHILD SUPPORT $_____

INTEREST INCOME $_____

INVESTMENT INCOME $_____

RENTAL INCOME $_____

OTHER INCOME $_____

TOTAL INCOME $_____

DEDUCT TOTAL EXPENSES $_____

UNCOMMITTED INCOME $_____

CASH FLOW STATEMENT

EXPENDITURES   Monthly

ORDINARY EXPENSES
- Regular Savings $ _____
- Food (include eating out) $ _____
- Clothing $ _____
- Child Care (Babysitting) $ _____
- Church Donations $ _____
- Club Dues $ _____
- Dentist $ _____
- Doctor or Health Care Costs $ _____
- Gifts (yearly / 12) $ _____
- Insurance Premiums $ _____
- Lottery Tickets $ _____
- Payments on Loans or Debts $ _____
- Personal Care Products $ _____
- Recreation and Holidays $ _____
- Subscriptions
    Cable T.V. and Hobbies $ _____
- Tuition or Education $ _____
- Union or Professional Dues $ _____

SHELTER
- Rent of Mortgage Payment $ _____
- Repairs and Improvements $ _____
- Taxes and Insurance (yearly /12) $ _____
- Telephone $ _____
- Utilities
    Gas/Oil and Electricity, Water $ _____

TRANSPORTATION
- Car Payment(s) $ _____
- Gas, Oil, Parking $ _____
- Insurance $ _____
- Licences (yearly /12) $ _____
- Maintenance and Repairs $ _____

MISCELLANEOUS EXPENSES $ _____

TOTAL EXPENSES $ _____

INSURANCE POLICIES

POLICY #1

Face Amount of Insurance $ _____
- Company _____
- Agent _____
- Type of Insurance _____
- Renewal Date _____
- Cash Surrender Value
  (if applicable) $ _____
- Premium $ _____

POLICY #2

Face Amount of Insurance $ _____
- Company _____
- Agent _____
- Type of Insurance _____
- Renewal Date _____
- Cash Surrender Value
  (if applicable) $ _____
- Premium $ _____

TOTAL AMOUNT OF INSURANCE

Policy #1 $_____
Policy #2 $_____
TOTAL   **$**_____

AUTO INSURANCE

- Company _____
- Agent _____
- Liability Amount $ _____
- Deductibles: 1. Comprehensive $ _____
                2. Liability $ _____
- Renewal Date _____

HOME/TENANT INSURANCE

- Home value $ _____
- Value of contents $ _____
- Company _____
- Agent _____
- Renewal Date _____

Record of Credit and Loans

	Amount	Payment	Int. Rate	Account #	Due Date
Mortgage					
Car Loan					
Line of Credit					
Credit Cards:					
Other Loans					

Financial Strategies For Women
ORDER FORM

Yes! I want to learn more about money, investments and how to increase my financial security.

	QTY		Total
Financial Strategies For Women:The Basics	____	$12.95	_____
Financial Strategies For Women: The Basics 90 minute audio cassette	—	$12.95	_____
Complimentary analysis of my Financial Review (Please send the completed forms from pages 160-167)		FREE	_____
Please include applicable taxes.			_____
For book or tape orders, add $3.00 shipping and handling.			_____
Discounts available for 10 books or more.		TOTAL	_____

Please send for details. Allow 4-6 weeks for delivery.

PLEASE PRINT
Name: _____
Address: _____
_____
City: _____ Province: _____
Postal Code: _____ Phone: _____

For your Financial Analysis please include the following information:
Present Age: _____ Years to Retirement: _____
Upon Retirement, would you have a Company Pension Plan? _____
Remember to include the completed forms from pages 160-167.

Send your cheque or money order to:
W.I.N. (Women's Investment Network) Inc.
981 Wellington Rd. S., Suite #402
London, Ontario N6E 3A9
Fax: (519) 649-6552